Yellow Tulips
on A
Cloudy Day

A Survivor's Journal

Christy Sims

ISBN-10 0998124400
ISBN-13: 978-0998124407

DEDICATION

To my mother, Elaine

My three amazing children – Chris and Elon, and Kayla – R.I.P

My brother, Anthony

The father of my children, Machon,

and my father, Thomas

I love you all infinitely. Your love saved me.

Project Editor: Jimisha Relerford
Book Cover Designer: Elaine Young, Hopscotch Communications

www.courageouschristy.com

Like many, I have been personally inspired by Christy's story, cheering from the sidelines as she was determined to fight to get her life back. As I know firsthand the strength of her support network, I was touched and honored when she asked me to write the foreword for this book. I met Christy when she was inducted into the National Coalition of 100 Black Women. Our spirits touched and agreed that we were in the right place doing great work in civic engagement for women and girls. We connected on a personal and professional level that secured our bond for life. Later when she would face the process of divorce, she trusted my perspectives on how to make the best of a bad situation.

The general rule is to begin a foreword by telling the reader what a book is about. As this book is about a person whose life was flipped upside down, I am going to flip the script and begin by telling you what this book is **_not_** about. This is not a book about domestic violence. In fact, as a behavioral scientist specializing in women and girls health, I approached my initial reading of Christy's book as an opportunity to look for clues and warning signs of unhealthy relationships that I could integrate into my messages to empower people to live their best lives. However, in a way that only Courageous Christy can, she flipped the script on me, and put me in the therapeutic seat where I had to completely own my status of "wounded healer". Yes, that is what this book _is_ about: Healing from the inside out in a way that results in taking back your power over all aspects of your life. This book is about confronting and fighting evil, injustice, and hate with truth, transparency, and defiance.

Courageous Christy pours her heart and soul into an unapologetic glimpse into a life full of a range of emotions of anger, sadness, depression, and outrage. In fact, she touched my unhealed wound when she described how her soul cried out. She cursed; she cried; she lashed out. She wanted answers that only God could provide as it relates to how someone who was doing everything she could to restore her life from a divorce, build her business, support her family, and contribute to her community, could experience such malicious behavior at the hands of someone who had once confessed his love......Oh wait—that's my story becoming one with

Christy's story! I promise you as you turn the pages of her personal journal and unfiltered accounts of her journey, you will find yourself in her words as she confirms we are all vulnerable to experiencing injustice that defies everything we believe God and humanity represents.

Christy's courage to write her story is uniquely penned to "un-silence" the suffering of survivors, many of whom have been quiet about the real turmoil, tension, conflict, and violence we face on a daily basis, but are afraid to disclose for fear of being judged as having made bad decisions. So we hide, deny, lie, and avoid the truth of the matter, which is "We all have secrets and shame as we seek to be loved." Well, what the devil meant for bad, God will get the glory as Christy is destined to force us to have the conversation about having more robust networks of trust and sister circles of accountability; and brothers who create barriers that cowardly batterers would never cross; and fix broken justice systems that would adequately punish perpetrators without re-traumatizing victims.

Yes, this book is about fighting for your life and future. Christy's honesty about love, sex, and God freed me in ways that allowed me to release all of my fears of future love based on my failed past relationships. As she fights to begin again, you will find yourself asking for forgiveness for feeling like you lacked anything. So, after my own soul cried out as only a wounded healer can relate, I drew up my tears and realized my courageous friend had given me at least six (6) core themes in her survivor's journal that touched me in ways that I will share with women and girls I meet everywhere:

1. *Healing is a process that cannot be rushed.*

2. *Children are stronger than we know and they are resilient in tragedy.*

3. *You can be "bitter" on your way to "better" as you commit to a renewed relationship with God.*

4. *Wounds leave scars that are constant reminders that you survived.*

5. *Trauma will force you to face whatever truths you have been avoiding.*

6. *Never let someone else's evil actions steal your joy, sense of humor, will to live, and capacity to love.*

Just as there was nothing in the world that could have prepared me to receive the news that my beautiful, talented, highly ambitious friend and colleague had been burned beyond recognition; in like manner, there is no length, depth, or content that this foreword could include that would prepare you for what you are about to experience as Courageous Christy takes you on a journey as only a survivor can. Be blessed as you take a deeper look into a brave soul that cried out, dried up, got up, and is ready to get on with her purpose-driven life!

Quinn M. Gentry. Ph.D., MBA
Behavioral Scientist, Author, & Executive Coach
President/CEO, Messages of Empowerment Productions
Atlanta, GA

Daily Mantra

I have fear, but fear does not have me

I have pain, but pain does not have me

I have anger, but anger does not have me

I have scars, but my scars do not have me

I Am free, I Am the Master of Me…

JOY IN THE MORNING

The day was April 28, 2013, a Sunday, and I was bouncing off of the walls with excitement and with the anticipation of new things to come. The four year storm had passed; I had graduated from Mercer University the previous December and I'd been working as a Mental Health and Substance Abuse Counselor for over a year. I was already a Nationally Certified Professional Counselor, and I had mailed my application to the state of Georgia to become a licensed Psychotherapist the previous Friday. My mother and I talked on the phone that day, chattering away and planning for my graduation ceremony and celebration scheduled for May 11th. I was so excited about the ceremony that I pressed my cap and gown in advance and I had been addressing my invites all morning. We come from very humble beginnings, my family. I am the first one of us to earn a Master's degree, so even though I was a 42 year old woman going back to finish school after 20 years away, and most of my classmates were young enough to be my children, my family was proud of me and insisted that I attend graduation. For the two years I had interned as a counselor during the day while attending classes at night and raising my children in the process. I was excited to *finally* be done, so that I could start to fulfill some of the promises that I'd made to my kids – promises to attend their sports games, to travel with them, to make up for all the time that we'd lost while I was studying and working.

I was a successful real estate broker for many years, but on that day, I was finally working in my calling as a counselor. I had stopped chasing money and started chasing joy; helping people that truly needed it brought me tremendous joy. The clients on my caseload at STAND Inc., the non-profit behavioral health organization where I worked, seemed to be clean and sober; they were rebuilding their lives, and some of them were making major breakthroughs in our therapy sessions. I was also rebuilding my life after a divorce. I was exercising, I was eating right, I was looking and feeling great, my kids were happy, and the bills were paid. Life was finally easy and peaceful.

My life was finally moving in the direction I wanted, but I still had one concern: my relationship with my boyfriend Drew, who was extremely jealous and possessive. I had begun to feel increasingly more controlled and manipulated by Drew, and my kids never liked him. I feared his reaction, but I had finally decided to end the relationship and move forward with my life. We were together all that weekend, but Drew could sense my resolve. He knew that I was finally done because I had become indifferent to him. I was so tired of his controlling and jealous behavior that I no longer wanted to be intimate with him, and I didn't care to argue with him anymore. I just wanted to be alone; I wanted peace. Drew watched me address my invitations for my graduation that morning, so he knew more than anyone how ecstatic I was to have finally finished something so challenging, but he didn't seem happy for me at all. In retrospect, I believe Drew viewed my step up the ladder of success as a step away from him.

I was happy that day. I was at peace with my life and at peace with my decision to leave Drew, but my peace was not to last. By 3 pm, I was in unthinkable agony. The bliss was no more – it was at that moment and on that day that my peaceful and happy life went awry. My life was forever changed on that day when my boyfriend, sensing that I was leaving the relationship, called me to the bathroom of my home and doused me with drain cleaner containing industrial grade sulfuric acid. I still cannot fully comprehend why he would want to hurt me in such a horrific way, but I believe he wanted to ensure that if he couldn't be with me, then neither would any other man, so he attacked the part of me that he thought was the most attractive: my outer appearance. I also believe that he used acid in particular not only to destroy my facial features, but my vision as well. He doused the chemical directly into my eyes and I was left blinded for several months. Of course, I can only speculate on his reasoning. I am not an evil person, and it is truly impossible for me to process the level of evil Drew embodied that day.

My last clear vision before losing my sight was of his reflection in the mirror standing behind me, watching me as I initially tried to rinse my eyes to relieve the burning. My eyes were the first to burn so I rushed from the hallway into the bathroom and began frantically rinsing my eyes with water. The more I rinsed, the more they seemed to burn. I was panicked, but he showed no emotion. He seemed completely calm as he stood there watching me. I saw a look in his eyes that day like none that I had seen before – the look of evil. He saw me panicking, yet made no attempt to help me until I screamed at him to call 911. It was as if my scream had snapped him out of him gaze.

I followed the sound of his movement down the hall and toward the kitchen. When I could go no further, I stopped and slid my body down the wall feeling helpless and confused. I didn't know what was in that bowl, but I could now feel the entire upper part of my body burning. I could no longer see or move, so I sat helplessly on the floor in my hallway, my back against the wall and my knees raised, in complete agony. I couldn't even open my eyes. I could feel the flesh burning on my face, my arms, my neck, and my chest. The pain was more intense, more brutal than the pain of all three of my children's births combined. I felt as if I were on fire and all I wanted was water. My body began to tremble, and I could barely breathe. In the back of my mind, I knew that I should get up and run to the shower or to the kitchen sink, but I could not move; I was paralyzed by the pain.

As I sat on the floor, I begged Drew to rinse me. I yelled at him. "What have you done? I hate you! I hate you!" I asked him what the 911 operator had told him, asked him why he was just standing there. "Why aren't you rinsing me? Put water on me, I'm burning! I can't open my eyes!" I screamed. Drew stood over me and said calmly, "Baby just sit here. They said if I rinse you the water will ignite the chemical." I didn't know what the chemical was, and I thought to myself, "What was in that bowl that could possibly be ignited by water?"

Drew and I had not argued, and I had no clue that he wanted to harm me, so I believed what he told me. I sat there…screaming, praying, hoping. I knew as I sat on the floor of my hallway that my life would never be the same again, but even in the midst of my agony, I could feel the presence of God. It was as if there was a holy presence hovering above me—sustaining me, calming me. I believed that I would not die. I could feel my flesh burning so I knew that I would be forever changed, but I had hope that I would survive that moment. I had hope that I would live to raise my kids.

Even in that hell, I had hope.

I thought of my children as I sat on that floor. Chris and Elon were scheduled to be back home around 4:30 that evening, so I knew that they

3

were likely already on the road with their father, Machon. It was not Machon's scheduled weekend to have them, but Chris had a baseball tournament in Savannah and he wanted to play in the tournament instead of attending his 8th grade prom. Chris has played baseball every year since he was four years old, and we've spent nearly every weekend at the baseball field most of his life. I would've preferred that he attend his prom, but he wanted to play in the tournament, so I let him go.

I couldn't hear my phone ringing through the sound of my own screams, but I found out later that the kids and their father had indeed been in the car on their way home. Chris told me that he'd called me nearly 20 times during the time that I sat there. He said that he could sense something was wrong, a feeling that was confirmed when a friend down the street texted him saying an ambulance and fire truck were parked at our house, and he was worried. Within the hour, Drew finally alerted my family that I was at the hospital and that I had been "accidentally" burned. I can only imagine what my kids were thinking – the fear that they must have felt. I can only imagine how long that drive from Savannah must have seemed to them. Machon told me later that he had to stop several times while on the road so he wouldn't cry in front of the kids. My mother had seen me by then and told him how badly I had been burned. He wanted to keep the kids calm.

I didn't find out until later that the chemical was sulfuric acid. When I finally heard the 911 tape months later, a chill went through my body, and I was enraged. The operator told Drew six times to rinse me. *Six times.* I sat in agony for what felt like an eternity before the ambulance arrived. I was a few feet away from the kitchen sink and only about 12 feet from the bathroom. Rinsing me off would've been so easy, and it could have changed the course of my life because I wouldn't have been permanently disfigured. Drew knew this. At one point during the call, he actually lied to the operator, insisting that he was rinsing me with soap and water. In actuality, he never rinsed the chemical off of me, in spite of my agonizing screams and his being advised to do so by the poison control operator. Even after dousing me, his conscience should have kicked in and he should've relieved me from the blinding pain. It never did, and his negligence led to me sustaining third and fourth degree burns to over 20 percent of my body. One hundred percent of my face was burned and disfigured. How could anyone be so evil and inhumane? How could I have cared for such a heartless monster?

"But the Lord stood with me and strengthened me, so that through me the proclamation might be fully accomplished, and that all the Gentiles might hear; and I was rescued out of the lion's mouth. The Lord will rescue me from every evil deed, and will bring me safely to His heavenly kingdom; to Him be the glory forever and ever. Amen." 2 Timothy 4:17-18

Henry County EMT finally arrived at my home. I was still sitting at the edge of my hallway in agony, but the sound of their voices gave me hope. When they asked Drew why he had not rinsed me, he replied, "Because the phone rang." I was confused by his response; I had begged him to rinse me, but he told me that he couldn't – that it would ignite the chemical.

I distinctly remember the weather being clear earlier that morning, but it must have shifted at some point during the day because the Atlanta Journal and Constitution reported that the heaviest and most torrential rainfall in all of 2013 occurred just as the ambulance was arriving at my house on April 28th, around 2:30 pm. By the time the paramedics arrived, I was burned so badly that they didn't have time to get me to the shower. The front door was closer, so they stripped my clothing, carried me outside, and rinsed me with rain water. My body trembled as the cold, heavy rain met my burned and open flesh. I could feel each rain drop piercing me like a zillion tiny knives, both agony and relief. The chemical had already burned through my flesh and to my bones, and it had burned through my chest to within 2 cm of my heart. If it had not been for the torrential rain that day and at that specific time, I wouldn't have survived. I know God did that.

After rinsing me as much as possible, the paramedics transported Drew and I to the Grady Burn Unit in Atlanta, Georgia. They bypassed at least five hospitals because they knew that I had the best chance of survival at Grady. For the duration of the ride to the hospital, Drew screamed that he was sorry and that it was an accident, and he kept complaining that he'd been burned also. I found out later that he sustained small burns on his arm, his back, and the top of his head, and was released from the hospital shortly after arriving. I was burned beyond recognition, although I was fully dressed; he was wearing only a pair of boxers, yet sustained no life altering injury.

The sound of Drew's voice caused me more distress because although I was in shock and did not understand why he did it, what the chemical was, or exactly how badly I was damaged, I could still feel the skin melting from my flesh. I knew within my soul that I would never be the same again – I just knew. I begged him to call my mom and my ex-husband because I knew my kids were on their way home and I wouldn't be there to receive them. Due to the trauma, my body and my mind went into shock, and I soon blacked out; I have no vivid memories of anything that happened that day after the ambulance ride.

My mother told me later that I was admitted to the Grady burn unit in critical condition. I learned later that I wasn't heavily sedated because within a few hours of arriving there, I was no longer experiencing pain. The absence of pain alerted the medical staff to how serious my injuries were, because when a burn victim feels no pain, it means that all nerve endings have been burned. Drew allowed the acid to sit on my skin so long that it burned down to my lower epidermis.

I also learned later that a Henry County investigator questioned me shortly after I arrived at the burn unit. I have no memory of being questioned, but apparently I repeated Drew's account that the acid attack was an accident. I cannot say why I said this, because I don't remember being questioned. My last memory is Drew screaming that it was an accident and that he was sorry. He said that he had slipped and fallen, but he never did. He did not slip and fall, because he was standing up right, directly in front of me when he doused me. Of that I am sure.

My brother went to my home the following morning to get my purse, cell phone, and laptop, and to retrieve some clothes for Chris and Elon. He also took several pictures while there. He later told me that as he stood there in the hallway of my home, he knew in that moment that it was not an accident. He described the scene as "unbelievable." There was splatter from the acid throughout the hallway and up the walls at least twelve feet outside of the bathroom. My laptop, which was on the bed when I left, was no longer there. My brother searched my home and the outside trash bin for the chemical and any evidence, but there was none; even the clothes the EMTs had stripped from my body had been taken away. Apparently, Drew had gone back to my home the day of the attack after leaving the hospital and cleared all visible evidence.

The incident occurred on April 28th, but I was told later by a Henry County police sergeant that Drew was not questioned until May 9th, two weeks after the attack. They believed his account of the incident, which I had apparently corroborated in the hospital, and filed the report as an accident. No law enforcement officers entered my home for an investigation until three months after the attack, when the incident was featured in the media. Henry County Crime Scene Investigators finally entered my home in mid-July of 2013, one month after I had awakened from the coma. By that time, I had lain in a coma for two months totally unrecognizable. My body was disfigured, my children no longer had their mother, and Drew had seemingly gone on with his life.

WHILE I WAS SLEEPING

At Grady, I was put into a medically induced coma because my brain nor my body could tolerate the pain of being burned so severely nor the pain from surgery. I had six life-saving skin grafting surgeries while I was in the coma. Due to the severity of my burns, I contracted multiple infections. The doctors did not expect me to survive. The skin from the front and back of my thighs served as donor sites to repair the skin on my neck, arms, and chest. My eyes were sewn shut to keep me from involuntarily opening them and causing further damage, so even if I'd wanted to open my eyes, I could not.

I could hear my mom talking about my graduation ceremony on May 11th, and although I was aware that Drew had caused me to miss it, in order to soothe myself I attended the graduation in my mind while lying in a coma. I envisioned that it was raining on that Saturday morning, so my graduation ceremony was moved from Mercer's outside lawn into the auditorium. I visualized myself proudly walking across the stage and shaking the hand of Dr. Caroline Brackette, my favorite professor, and then receiving my degree from Dr. Williams, the Director of the Counseling department at Mercer. Strangely, my mom was not at my imaginary graduation. It may be because she was actually sitting next to me in the hospital room, and thus my mind did not transport her there with me. At any rate, the graduation within my mind was wonderful. I did whatever possible to sustain myself mentally and to not give up and die. I wanted to live, I wanted to see my babies grow up, and I wanted to tell my story.

The human brain is indeed magnificent. My mind saved my life while I was in a coma. I have always wondered what being in a coma feels like, and now I know. Being in a coma is a strange and scary phenomenon, yet it was also peaceful sometimes. I believe that I was in a dreamlike state most of the time, but there were times when I was aware and could hear people talking, nurses and doctors working, babies crying in other rooms. I dreamt of my grandmother, Dorothy, whom I loved dearly. She came to comfort me, and we laughed and went for long walks. She was dressed in all white and looked exactly as she did when she died when I was 7 years old. I loved her so much and her presence comforted me while lying there.

I dreamt of my aunt, Sherrell and she looked just as she did on her wedding day, which was the last time that I saw her before she was killed in a car explosion on her honeymoon. She was dressed in a lavender tea-length dress, with a flowered head band in her hair. She smiled the entire time that I was with her; we sat and talked for hours and she told me that I should find joy in every little thing. She said that joy was the most important thing in life, and that nothing mattered if there was no joy in it.

I dreamt that I was with my uncle Billy when he passed from cancer, and that I was able to say goodbye to him. My daughter Kayla, who passed away in 2001, has always come to me in my dreams, so it was no surprise that I dreamt of her often. I held her in my arms for hours and hours in my dreams, and she brought me so much peace and joy while lying there. I thank God for that coma, because He allowed me to sleep my way through hell.

While lying in a coma, I planned Chris' fourteenth birthday party, I sold my house, I wrote an entire book, I redecorated a new house, I went to visit my job at STAND and talked to my boss, Mr. Sperling, I counseled a few clients, I drove my car. I went to Hawaii. I could hear Elon laughing and see Chris skateboarding. Later, when I discussed this in counseling, my therapist explained that I was likely not always dreaming. Since I was in a medically induced coma, my brain was fully functional, and I could often hear talking and music in my room. Still, in order to survive two months of being immobile and unable to see or talk, of stillness, of entrapment within my own body, of loneliness, of fear, I had to disassociate, just as people who experience trauma and abuse do. I continued to take meditative trips within my mind. I was determined to wake up and be with my children again. I imagined us playing at the beach, happy and whole again. I went into the deepest dream state after each surgery and would stay there for days because the medication was so strong. I'm guessing that it was Morphine or some other type of hallucinogen because my dreams were so strange and vivid during those times, and they seemed to last for days after each surgery. My days were endless – I never knew what time it was, if it was night or day, what I looked like, who was touching me, what nurse was on duty, or who was walking into the room until I learned their voices or the smell of their perfume.

My constant while lying in a coma was thoughts of Chris and Elon, who were my greatest concern. My comfort was the sound of my mother's voice praying and saying that she loved me, and the sound of gospel music playing non-stop. My mother requested that the nurses never leave me alone in silence, so the gospel station played on the radio 'round the clock for two months. Every time the song "A God Like You" by Kirk Franklin played, I would dance in my mind, and even now when I hear that song, I smile and rejoice and dance no matter where I am, simply because I can. I woke up knowing the words to every gospel song on the radio and now I wake up every day with a song in my head and on my heart. Music soothed me and made me feel connected to the outside world while lying there.

I could hear and feel the presence of my father there. Sometimes he would come to my room and just sit beside me without ever saying a word, other times I could hear him weeping. I could hear my brother, Quinn praying and crying. I wanted to wake up to comfort him, but I could not. I could feel Machon holding my hand every night. He worked all day, then went home to care for our kids, and he would then come to the hospital to check on me late at night before going to bed. He later said that it was easier going home to the kids and easier for him to sleep knowing that he had seen me. I never wanted to let him go because I loved him, because I felt safe when he was there, and because his presence made me feel connected to our kids. I wanted to tell them all so badly how much I loved and appreciated them, and how sorry I was for causing them so much pain. I felt loved while lying in that coma. It is the pure and unconditional love from my family that motivated me to live. *They* never gave up on me, so *I* never gave up on me.

I resumed planning Chris' birthday party every time I could hear them preparing me for another surgery because it was a pleasant thought to ease the anxiety before the anesthesia kicked in. I planned a Hawaiian themed pool party and cookout. I invited everyone in the family and all of his friends. It was colorful and festive, and there was plenty of food. His dad was on the grill cooking as usual. I have never seen Chris so happy, and it made me smile. I gave him birthday parties every year when he was very young, but he doesn't remember any of them. I wanted him to have a party that he would remember, one that everyone would remember. In my dreams, I succeeded, and it was a lovely day.

While lying there for two months, I could not move or see, but I could hear and feel everything – every touch, every needle, every prick. There was no pain, but I could feel it. I felt trapped within my own body. I wanted to scream that I could hear and feel them. I wanted to get up and walk right out of that hospital and go home to my babies, but I had to lay there in the stillness and darkness. Every time I heard a man's voice I clinched, my heart pounded, and my blood pressure rose. I wondered if it was him...

I finally awoke from the two-month coma in mid-June of 2013, still bandaged and unaware of the actual damage that had been done to me. Dr. Walter Ingram, the acute burn surgeon at Grady who saved my life and managed my care, advised my mom to remove me from the burn unit and send me to rehab at Emory University Hospital in Atlanta. He said that he had done all that he could do for me, and if I stayed in the burn unit any longer, I would possibly lose hope. He said that I needed to start moving again. I awoke from the coma unable to move my arms or legs. The nerves in my arms were affected by the acid, I was completely blind at this point, I was immobile from the waist down, and I was unable to speak due to a tracheotomy that had been in my throat to assist my breathing. I needed intense rehabilitation before I could resume my life.

On the day I left Grady Hospital, the nurses gathered around me as I was rolled out of the burn unit. I could hear some of them weeping as I was rolled away. They wished me well and assured me that I would be okay. I wish I could have seen their faces, and I wish that I could have spoken and said "thank you." I have never laid eyes on any of them, but I felt like I knew them because I had heard their voices for two months and I knew their scents. They hugged my mom and said goodbye.

ANGELS IN THE VALLEY

I arrived at the Emory Rehabilitation Center conscious and aware, but completely broken. I had lost 40 pounds from being on a feeding tube for two months while in the coma; I was so frail. I had been trying to lose weight for months, but this was certainly not the way that I'd wanted to lose it. I had not seen my kids since I dropped them off for school on April 26th, and I wondered if I would ever be able to lay eyes on them again. I tried to remember what they were wearing that last day because I wanted to hold on to that memory. All I remember is saying goodbye to them, but I hope I told them that I loved them as well.

I had only been awake from the coma for two days when they transferred me to Emory for rehab. I was afraid of entering this new environment without being able to see, walk, talk, or move my arms. I couldn't feed or bathe myself, or even turn myself over in the bed. I felt like an infant. I was totally helpless and dependent upon total strangers for my every need. I wondered if they would treat me well. I wondered how long I would be there. I was afraid that I would never be able to care for my children again. I was afraid of seeing my own face for the first time. I was afraid of being

11

alive. I was afraid that I would never be the woman that I once was. I was afraid of the unknown. I was so afraid…

Strangely, I'd felt safer within the confines of the coma.

Once I was awake, I could no longer dream and take meditative trips. This was real; it had happened. He did this on purpose – he tried to burn me alive. He said that he slipped and fell, but he never did. He was standing right in front me. It happened so fast that I didn't have time to react, and soon after everything went black. But why? I was backing away from the relationship. I had told him weeks prior that I could not marry him, but we never argued that day. What did I do to deserve this? Did I say something to trigger him that morning? I remembered everything. Why was he only wearing boxers? Why was he clearing the tub drain when it was working perfectly? We had used that bathtub all weekend, and I had taken a shower just hours before and the drain was not clogged. Why did he put drain cleaner in my cereal bowl? How did I not see him doing any of this? When did he buy the chemical?

After a few days of being at Emory I began to adjust. I got to know some of the most incredible people with beautiful spirits while in rehab at Emory. My two roommates during that time were Ola Maye Jackson and Sue Harris Vaughan. I grew to love them both. They made me laugh when I felt like crying. They lied to me and told me that I was beautiful every day before I saw my face. They became attached to my mom. They could not believe how devoted Machon was to my care, and after being divorced for so many years, I could not believe the extent of his grace either. They were impressed by him and they predicted that we would get back together. We ordered pizza to our hospital room and did everything possible to make our stay more bearable. Our room was the life of the fourth floor because although none of us could walk, and we were all dealing with our own individual suffering, we all had strong and vibrant personalities, and we kept the nurses on their toes. We all left within a week of each other, but I was the only one that walked out of the rehab center. Ola Maye suffered from spine cancer, and she never walked again. She ultimately passed away in August 2014. Sue is now walking and thriving, and we keep in touch via social media.

The phlebotomist, Danita, who took my blood every day has now become a lifelong friend. The Chaplain, Janet, and I developed a spiritual connection that is difficult to explain. She came to my room and talked to me whenever she could. There was a light around her that I could feel, although I could not see her. She prayed with me. She told me that I was still beautiful, and I desperately wanted to believe her because I still hadn't seen my face. We talked about everything. She said that being around me was a blessing to her and that she could see God's power working through me. She marveled at the level of my faith and belief in God. She was amazed by the commitment of my mother, my father, my brother, and Machon. I know for certain that Janet was an angel sent by God to comfort me during that dark time. I have tried to locate her, but I have neither seen nor heard of her since my time with her at Emory.

I loved the staff that cared for me at both Grady and Emory, but I had more awareness at Emory. They were my angels in the valley, my yellow tulips on a cloudy day. They cared for me when I could not care for myself, and I will never forget any of these incredible souls. I received daily physical and occupational therapy at Emory. I was determined to go home without a wheelchair, so I worked harder than I was asked to. If Abby, my physical therapist, asked me to take 20 steps with my walker, I would push myself to take 40 steps. I didn't know if I would ever get my sight back, but I was determined to regain the use of my arms and legs. Within a month, I was walking, I was bathing myself with assistance, and I was feeding myself. The food at Emory was so good, and I was allowed to eat all that I wanted because I needed to gain some of the forty pounds that I had lost. The highlights of my days were breakfast, lunch, and dinner!

One of my nurses, Regina, reminded me what it is like to walk in your purpose. Regina shared with me how she knew at four years old that she wanted to be a nurse. It was obvious that this was her calling, and that she truly enjoyed being a nurse. She was so nurturing and so loving, and she requested to take care of me whenever she was on duty. All of the nurses at Emory were fantastic, but Regina and I developed a special bond. Before I could bathe myself, she would bathe me and care for me as if I were a new born baby. I remember crying one night as she bathed me because I had so much pride and I did not like being taken care of by a relative stranger. I felt so helpless...and hopeless. Regina said that it was her pleasure to take care of me. She told me that as a mother I had nurtured my babies when they couldn't care for themselves. She said that everyone at some point in their life would have to be cared for like this, and this was just a temporary thing. She said that I would one day have my health back and I would live to nurture and care for someone else. She said that she loved her job as a nurse, that it was a blessing to care for people, and she told me to dry my eyes and let her do the job that God had called her to do. She washed my hair and dressed me, and I fell asleep.

I awakened the next morning more humble and with less pride. I learned that night not to rob another person of the blessing of giving. I learned that it is arrogance to believe that I should always be the one in the position of giving. I learn to just say thank you and let it be.

I will never forget Regina for as long as I live. When I left Emory, I said that I never wanted to be there again, so I never went back for outpatient therapy as I was instructed. I think I'm ready to go back now. I believe that it would bring Regina joy to see how far I have come. I want to see my angel nurse again, to hug her and say thank you again.

I saw my face for the first time while at Emory. I asked a nurse who did not normally care for me to give a mirror and she complied. I knew that I had been burned terribly, but I had hope that I would be okay. I was *not* okay. As I looked into the mirror and I gasped, my heart dropped. I felt as if someone had just punched me in the chest. The only thing that compares to the way I felt is the moment that I learned that my baby, Kayla, had passed away. My vision wasn't yet clear, but I could tell that this thing in the mirror was not *me*. My hair had been cut off, I was completely bald. My left eye appeared to be inches lower than my right eye. My entire face was burned and swollen. My complexion was three shades darker. I could not see my nose. Where was my nose?! I screamed, "What the hell did he do to me?!" It was so much worse than I had imagined. I looked like a monster, and I didn't see how it could ever be fixed or how I could ever be pretty again. This is when the grieving process began. As long as I did not see myself, I had hope. The nurse consoled me as I began to weep out loud. I wish that my mother or someone who knew and loved me had been there. I felt as if someone that I loved dearly had died, and that someone was me. I was pretty no more…

I became deeply depressed, and there were many days when I wanted to give up. I cried myself to sleep most nights. My mom, my dad, my brother, Machon, Ola Mae, Sue, Regina, and Janet were my comforters; they kept me lifted. I had not seen my children in over two months, but thoughts of them made me want to live. Machon would tell me all the details of their days; they were out for the summer and Chris' team was headed to the world series. I imagined his excitement, in that moment, I would have given anything to see my son play baseball. Elon was going to tumbling classes during the summer and Machon gave me a play by play of her progress. He was my connection to my babies. I wondered if they missed me as much as I missed them. I wondered if their hearts ached and if they cried themselves to sleep every night the way that I cried myself to sleep every night because I missed them so much. Their dad did everything in his power to keep them so busy and active that they didn't have much time to be sad. I had no clue how they were truly doing, but Chris and Elon were my driving force. I could not leave my children in this world without a mother, so I continued with my therapy. I cried every day, and I prayed. When it was too much to bare, I did what my mother had taught me to do – I called upon the name of Jesus. There is indeed power in His name.

A NEW FIGHT

My family had been pleading with the Henry County police department to investigate my case. Once I awakened from the coma and I was lucid enough to give an accurate statement, my family asked them to come to Emory to question me, but they never did. A family friend and attorney, Odis Williams, came to my hospital room at Emory and recorded my statement, then delivered it to the police; still there was no action. While Odis was working for me on the legal end, my brother Anthony and my two best friends, Jonell Myers and LaNese Harris, began telling people about my tragedy and started the Courageous Christy/Justice for Christy Movement to help me seek justice, create awareness about what Drew had done to me, and raise money. They started a website and began raising money in support of my reconstruction and recovery process. The support of our friends, the Atlanta community, and people from throughout the country was amazing. The media soon became interested in my story and things finally began to move forward. We all suspected then that this was the beginning of something very challenging, but truly extraordinary. Team Courageous Christy originally included my brother, Anthony, Machon, Jonell, LaNese, Dr. Cherry Collier, Shanti Das, Crystal Drake, and Joseph David Smith. They all conferenced called weekly with the specific task of helping me rebuild my life. Everyone should be so blessed to have an entire team of people conspiring on their behalf; I am forever grateful for their love and support.

I "walked" out of Emory on July 11, 2013 with about 50 percent of my vision and 50 percent use of my arms, and looking like something from "Tales from the Crypt." I was totally unrecognizable and in no position to be out in public, especially without a veil. Still, I was determined to speak my truth.

I went immediately to the Henry County Police Department to file an accurate police report. In spite of the obvious damage that was done to me, the police seemed totally disinterested, but they processed the report. My family and friends had been calling the police department the entire time that I was lying in a coma, begging them to investigate my case, but they had already filed it as an accident. I didn't realize that I had already given a formal statement to the police on that first day of the attack. As I said, I have no memory of being questioned, and no one ever told me that I had already given a formal statement, so I gave my statement after leaving rehab thinking that it was all they needed to arrest Drew. Unfortunately, there was still no progress in the case until my story was reported in the media in mid-July. Tom Reagan of Channel 2 Action News and the radio station V-103 were the first to report my story. At that point, there was still only awareness and a public uproar; there was no arrest. My life had been turned upside-down, and Drew still walked free.

My family, my friends, and now the media began to call the Henry County Police Department asking questions. I grew impatient as I lived in total discomfort and total isolation, wondering if I would ever be able see clearly again, if I would ever have a normal life. As each day went by, we all grew angrier that we were suffering while he went on with his life. I finally could not take it anymore, so I asked my brother to take me back to the police department so I could meet with Detective Brand, the officer handling my case. I had spoken with him a few times over the phone, but I needed him to see my burned and disfigured face – I needed him to be affected enough to take action. I thought to myself, "Maybe he doesn't understand how bad this is…how could anyone see how much damage this man did to twenty percent of my body and still believe this was an accident?"

My brother and I arrived at the police department in late July. We initially met with an officer to give a theft report because my laptop and a few other items were missing from home, and since they would not arrest Drew for assaulting me, we hoped that filing a report for the theft would at least prompt them to question him again. After speaking with a female officer, we requested to see Detective Brand. My vision was still not clear at this time, and I was veiled and wearing sunglasses. Nevertheless, Detective Brand just sat there smugly looking at me. He began to question me as if I was the one who had thrown acid in someone's face. He said that I'd told him that first day that it was an accident and that I seemed perfectly fine and lucid when I said it. My heart dropped; I hadn't known until that moment that Detective Brand was the officer who questioned me that first day. I had talked to this man several times, and I had encountered him the day that I filed the police report, but not even my mother told me that he was the officer at the hospital the first day at Grady. I had no memory of ever seeing this guy or giving him a statement, and I was totally shocked when he told me, as he sat leaning on the back of his chair-looking at me with total indifference. I knew then that he didn't believe me – I could see it in his eyes. I walked right out of the police department and went directly to the District Attorney's office. It all made more since now…why would this detective who didn't investigate my case or ever even enter my home in the beginning believe that my ordeal was anything other than an accident? It was as if he was totally unaffected by my suffering. He saw how badly I was burned, and he didn't seem to care. I can only imagine the atrocities he sees daily as a cop, but I would never want a job that would cause me to become so jaded to human suffering. How could any human being see this level of inhumanity and not be outraged?

We arrived at the DA's office which is housed inside of the Henry County Courthouse. We did not have an appointment, but my brother and I were determined not to leave without speaking to the Assistant DA, Sandi Rivers. We had heard from Odis Williams, our attorney friend who had taken my videotaped statement to the police weeks prior, that Sandi Rivers was a fair and honest woman, that she was experienced and smart, and that she was a police detective for many years prior to being the ADA. We sat and prayed that she would see us that day because I knew that I could no longer count on the police department to get justice, and I could not bear going back to my isolated room in my mom's house without making some progress that day.

Finally, the clerk came in and said that Mrs. Rivers would see us. Getting in to see her without an appointment felt like a miracle to me, a sign of things to come. I knew instinctively in that moment that this woman would be the catalyst for change that we so desperately needed. I knew that this day would not be in vain. I prayed that she would see and hear me and know that I was telling the truth.

Sandi Rivers walked into the room and sat down at a conference table with us. She listened patiently as I told my story. She seemed empathetic, and she asked more questions than I had ever been asked by the police in the past few weeks. I could see her detective experience in the questions that she asked. She asked questions that not even I had thought of—if Drew went back to my house the evening of the assault, who picked him up from the hospital, since he'd ridden with me in the ambulance? Why did he leave Grady so abruptly knowing that the police wanted to question him? Why would he leave me there in critical condition, not knowing if I would live or die? Why was it so important for him to get back to my house so quickly? Where did he dispose of the evidence? Why not just put it in my outside trash bin? Why put it in his car and take it away from my house? Why would anyone put drain cleaner in a cereal bowl? His girlfriend is possibly dying and his first thought is to go back to the house and clean up?

The ADA was already investigating the case right there in that conference room. A peace came over me when she looked me into my eyes, touched my shoulder and said, "I believe you, Christy…I believe you're telling the truth." She comforted me further by saying, "In spite of what this man has done to you, I can still see your beauty. Please know that the outside really doesn't matter." I looked like a monster, and that mattered very much to me, but I appreciated her kindness and knew then that she would do what was right. She remained professional and objective, but I could feel her compassion and empathy – she asked if she could give me a hug as we left. I slept peacefully that night for the first time since I woke up from the coma. The case was officially reopened and, as I said, the Henry County CSI entered my home for the first time three months after the assault.

MY SOUL CRIED OUT

By mid-July, I was back at my mom's house, sleeping in my old room. Depression had set in fully, and I was crying every day. I missed the comfort of my own home, but I couldn't go to my home in Henry County just yet because I couldn't care for myself or my kids. I knew that Drew still walked free, so I wasn't sure if it was safe for my family there. I couldn't go out in public without a veil. I would need months of physical and occupational therapy to restore my body's functionality, and I was legally blind. My vision was blurred, I had no peripheral vision in my left eye at all because of damage to the eyelid, and some mornings when I woke up I couldn't see at all. I didn't know if I would ever be able to see my babies' faces clearly again. I didn't know if I would ever be able drive them to school again, cook for them, or watch their games. My life was so uncertain, and I didn't know how to handle it.

What a blessing it is to have close friends who are also counselors. It is not by happenstance that I became a counselor at STAND, Inc. and encountered my friends Francis, Warren, and Mr. Sperling prior to this tragedy. God is the best of knowers, and His timing is always perfect. My co-workers were all helpful to me in their own way throughout my ordeal. Francis encouraged me to journal my thoughts, and he left two journals in my mom's mailbox one day. Although my vision was not yet clear, it was time for me to start back writing.

The last time I'd written consistently was twelve years prior when my daughter, Kayla passed away. The pain I felt after the attack was very different, but nearly as deep. Sometimes in life, the pain is so deep that the mouth simply cannot form the words to articulate it; it is then that we should write them down. Edward P. Morgan said, "A book is the only place in which you can examine a fragile thought without breaking it, or explore an explosive idea without fear it will go off in your face. It is one of the few havens remaining where a man's mind can get both provocation and privacy." My thoughts were indeed fragile, and I used this premise to explore this pain that I couldn't adequately express with the spoken word. It is easier for me to express myself in writing, and I knew that I must express my emotions in order to move forward and heal. And so I decided, as the words flowed from me onto the page like water, that I would write until the pain is no more.

Monday July 15, 2013

It has been four days since I left the hospital and arrived at my mom's house, and I am still legally blind. I can write these words, but I can barely read them back to myself. Lord, thank you for my life and for the opportunity to live another day. I am broken, I am nearly blind, but I am alive. Thank you in advance for my complete healing. I am feeling down today. I am morning my former face, my former body, and my former life. I know that this is all happening to glorify you Lord, but it is more than I can bear. Please forgive me for moments of doubt. You are my strength and my redeemer and I know that all things are possible through You. Please give me the strength and endurance to deal with this new life, and please also give it to my family. Lord please send your protective angels to be about my children while I am away from them. Please guard their hearts and their minds.

Lord, how could You let this happen to me? I thought that I was doing Your work. I'm pissed off! Why me?! This is too much for me. Please heal me and make me whole again. I am so depressed. I miss my babies, my home, my beauty, my job, my good health, my happiness, my peace. I was happy Lord! I thought that I had made it through the storm. Please reveal to me what You want me to learn from this tragedy. Allow me to glorify You, but please don't let me suffer too long.

I am weary. I feel angry, depressed, and doubtful at times. I am sore and uncomfortable, and my body aches all over. I feel ugly, broken, and dependent. I hate this existence! Lord, I need relief! It has been raining for weeks and I am actually thankful for the rain because it is in alignment with my depressed mood. If it were sunny outside, I would be more pissed off because I can't go outside. Holy Spirit please lift me up and give me peace.

Tuesday July 16, 2013

In spite of it all, I am grateful for my ability to walk, my amazing mother, my kids, my brother, Machon, dad, Francis, Warren, a great boss in Mr. Sperling, good health insurance, for my improving vision. I am thankful for all the prayers of friends and strangers, for good food, for a warm comfortable place to heal, for the possibility of reconstructive surgery, for the hope that I can be whole again. Lord, I thank You for the ability to finally use my right hand so that I can write and care for myself. Thank you for this journal so I can express my thoughts. Lord, I thank you for brief moments of peace and stillness. I am comforted by memories of Chris and Elon playing on the beach when they were younger. Memories are all I have right now. Thank you for those memories.

Saturday July 20, 2013

Lord, I am trusting You to get me through this. I am looking forward to a full recovery. I slept until noon today. I am better when I am asleep because I don't have to think about what has happened to me. I spoke with Machon when I first woke up today and he gave me some hope about reconstructive surgery. He researched and found a doctor in Baltimore who specializes in burn reconstruction. I believe that seeing some before and after photos of other burn survivors may give me more hope. I'm still depressed, but I'm feeling better than yesterday. I also spoke to Jonell and she expressed how many people want to help me. It is harder to give up when I have so many people that truly care about me. I have love flowing through me and around me at all times. Chris' 14th birthday is in three days and he wants to come and spend it with me. The kids are living with their dad downtown at his condo in Atlantic Station and they seem to be doing as well as can be expected. I have yet to see Elon and it is breaking my heart. We speak daily and she seems to be having fun taking tumbling classes and hanging out with her cousins during the summer, but she is my baby, my pudding pie, and I worry about her all day, every day. I miss them both so much.

Based on spiritual theology, we have free will as both humans and spirits, and thus there is a possibility that some of our life events are planned on a soul level before we get here, and if that is so then there must be a plan for me to get through this tragedy and learn from it. Lord, I know that this was not Your doing because You are a loving and just God – a God of compassion. This was the work of evil, because You allow free will. But I also know that You have the power to fix all this. My complete healing, both internally and externally, is in the power of Your divine hands, and I'm counting on You to get me through this hell on earth.

Wednesday July 24, 2013

Chris' 14th birthday was yesterday. I planned the most elaborate birthday party while lying in that coma. I wish I could have given him one in real life, but I am confined to my mom's house right now. I only go out in public to doctor's appointments.

It was nice having Chris with me this week for his birthday. We just hung out and watched TV mostly. I felt bad about him spending his birthday with me instead of his friends, but it was his birthday and he insisted. I can see the pain in his eyes, but he is so mature and caring. Our roles are now reversed at times. I find that he has now become my comforter. My fourteen year old son prays like an eighty year old minister; he has always been anointed with the gift of prayer and we pray together often. Chris never liked Drew and I wish that I had listened to him years ago. He was never good for me, but I truly did not see this coming. Being hurt to this level is unreal. I still can't believe the damage to my face and body. It's like I'm living within an unending nightmare. I wake up every day hoping that this was just a horrible dream.

Lord, I know that I will get through this, but who will I be and what will I look like on the other side? Will I ever be happy again? I thought that I was through the storm and headed in the right direction. Why now? Why this? Why me? This hit me like a brick and its taking all the emotional fortitude that I have to stay sane.

Thank You Lord for dwelling within me. It is the only reason that I am not totally crazy and suicidal right now. I see Your Spirit in all the people around me. I have been surrounded by kindness throughout this ordeal and I know that it is your Divine Order. I recognize You, Lord even on my darkest days. I will glorify Your name and I be a living testimony to Your healing power. People will witness my recovery and change as a result of it. I will live a purpose driven life. I will travel, live, and love again. This is only temporary, I know that You allowed me to live for Your glory, and I know that You will not allow me to stay this way. Let Your will be done concerning Drew and remove all hatred and bitterness from my heart so that there is only room there for me to love.

You have given me so many gifts that I still need to share with others. I'm looking forward to a better life than I had before. Lord, please allow me to bless others through this tragedy. Continue to infuse me with strength and courage so I can heal others as I heal myself.

Thursday July 25, 2013

I feel dead inside. I feel alone, and I am uncomfortable every moment of the day. This suffering is lasting too long and no one understands. I'm missing the kids and I want to go upstairs and fall into my mama's arms but I can't complain to her because she is already heartbroken; I have already put her through too much. I can't let her see me crying. So, it's just You and me, God.

I have a radio interview with Ryan Cameron on V-103 in the morning, so I'm going to bed soon so I'll feel rested, and so I can forget the pain. I have no clue what I'm going to say in the morning. This is my first radio interview and it will be aired live. Ryan Cameron is the top radio personality in Atlanta, and there will be over a million people listening to me sharing the most horrific event of my life. Quinn will be in the studio with Ryan, and I will be calling into the studio from home. Please give us both the right words Lord, let us be clear and concise; allow the truth to flow from our lips and for our words to glorify You in all that we say.

I love You Lord, but I'm so angry at You right now!

Saturday July 27, 2013

I did the V-103 and WAOK interviews, and I believe that they both went fairly well. The Channel 2 News interview has been airing all day. I'm not thrilled with the way I was presented on TV. They edited some pivotal and impactful parts of that interview. I was completely in shadow and I don't think it had much impact. People won't be able to grasp what has been done to me. I hate that they showed the hideous scars on my arms. I hate being in this situation, but suffering in silence is not healthy for me. People need to know what has happened. I am amazed at the response from the V-103 interview. It is nice to know how many people care about me. I am shocked by the number of donations from complete strangers. It is a beautiful display of the goodness of people in the midst of so much evil and inhumanity. I am in the deepest part of my valley. I can see no way out of this. My face is gone; I am no more. I feel isolated and invisible. A part of me died that day – the part of me that trusts and loves unconditionally died right there in that hallway; it never made it the hospital.

I wake up every day longing to go back to sleep because I am still her in my dreams. I don't want to be this helpless and broken person. I have been strong and independent all of my life. I don't know how to be this new person. I can barely see, I have no face, and I am unrecognizable. How can I function in this cruel world in this condition? Who will ever love me or desire me? How will I work and support my children? I don't feel like a person at all, I feel like a *thing* that is burdening my family. I can imagine the pain in their eyes when they look at me. I can especially feel the helplessness of the men in my family, including my son. My grief is compounded by this awareness of their grief. The pieces of my broken heart feel like twenty pound weights. I am angered by the audacity, and I am heartbroken by the inhumanity. I feel hollow, and the lump in my throat is so large that I am finding it hard to swallow my own saliva. He has succeeded; that bright light inside of me has faded. My soul is dark and my spirit is weak. I have no joy; nothing pleases me but the sound of my children's voices, and even that is bittersweet because I cannot go home to them. I cannot adequately care for them. I have survived many things, but I cannot see my way through this. My heart, my body, and my entire life has been shattered into a million little pieces, and I have no clue how to put them back together again. I cannot see beyond this moment. I literally cannot see as far as my own toes. Sleep is my only escape, and lately even that eludes me. I need You, Lord. I need the solace that only You can provide. Please ease this pain.

Mom's antique Coca Cola rotary dial house phone rings louder than fire trucks racing to a four alarm fire. It annoys me to a level that I cannot express. I'm thankful that she and Bill take such good care of me and that I have a quiet and peaceful place to heal, but a rotary phone in 2013? Living here again feels like being trapped in a time warp. My mom has everything in her house that she had when I was ten years old. I'm watching the same TV that I raced home from school to watch the Jetson's and the Flintstones on when I was a kid. I'm sleeping in my same bed. Anyway, the phone woke up me up out of a much needed sleep. After praying and crying for hours, I guess that I had finally drifted off to sleep. The sound of the phone annoyed me, but I didn't answer it because it is not my phone and I rarely get any calls here. Bill yelled out to me to pick up the phone, and I reluctantly answered it. My inner voice whispered, "Who the hell is this?"

The voice on the other end was familiar, nearly as familiar as the sound of my own voice because it was the voice of someone that I once cared for deeply. He knew me when I was young and beautiful. He said that he heard me on the radio yesterday and wanted to see how I was doing. I forgot to ask him how he got my mom's number. It caught me off guard that he called on the house phone because only a few people have this number, but I was so elated to hear his voice that I didn't care how he found me. I have thought of him often, and I have tried to locate him many times over the years. I have not seen or spoken to him in over twenty years, but strangely talking to him brought me peace that I cannot explain. During our talk I had no thoughts or worries of the past nor of the future. I dwelled in that moment. Talking to him felt natural; it was as if he has been here all along. There was no awkwardness nor need to catch up on lost time. It was as if time had stood still for us all these years. He didn't ask me any evasive questions as people often do. His only question was, "How are you really, my little CJ?" I smiled within my soul because these words transported me back in time, back to a time when I was young and free. In that moment I realized that he is still the only one on the planet that calls me CJ. Only a few people know that my middle name is Jenean because when I got married to Machon and my last name became Sims, I legally replaced my middle name with Tucker. He asked again, "How are you really, my little CJ?" I blushed and replied, "I am better now."

Amazingly, I still feel connected to him after all these years. His voice was soothing and kind. I could hear sincerity, empathy and compassion in his voice. We talked for hours about everything and nothing. He prayed for me, we ended our call and I slept deeper that night than I have in days. I guess that God sent me someone who knew me back when to remind me of who I was, and of who I still am. I survived another day...

Sunday July 28, 2013

Chris has been visiting often, but Elon finally saw me for the first time yesterday since I dropped her off at school on April 26th, three months ago. My face is so messed up, I look like a creature from the crypt. I honestly don't look human and not having any hair makes it worst. I missed Elon so much, but I felt guilty that she had to see me this way. Their dad brought them over and we sat and talked for an hour. I could tell that she's gotten taller, but I could not make out the details of my baby girl's face. I had to pretend that I could see her clearly. I told her how beautiful she is, just as I have almost every day of her of life. It took all the strength that I had not to grab her and hold her tightly and never let her go. My baby was finally brave enough to see me. I wanted to break down and cry, but she has been afraid to see me all this time, and it's taken several counseling sessions to get her ready for this moment, so I didn't want to make her emotional. Instead, I made her laugh as much as possible. We talked about random brainless stuff like her favorite TV shows, her hair, and just whatever to keep our minds off of the fact that I now look liked Freddy Krueger. I acted as if I was completed normal, and I could tell that she was pretending also, and that she didn't want to upset me by crying. I have waited three months to see this beautiful and sweet child, and now she was standing right in front of me and I could barely see her. God, please make this better.

I have brave, unselfish, and extraordinary children. They both have done well in my presence, but Machon said that the moment that they left me last night—Elon cried for hours and hours and he was unable to console her. I feel awful about upsetting her last night. I haven't seen her in months and now I've probably emotionally scarred her for life. I should have waited a little longer to see her; it was too soon and I should have worn a veil. Chris is hurting, but Elon is a more sensitive and emotional child. I can only hope that it gets better and that they become stronger and more empathetic. I just hate that it had to be this way. I despise him for what he has done to my babies and to my entire family. They deserve better. I deserve better. This has devastated everyone around me; I can see the pain in their eyes and I'm pissed off about it. I hope he rots in hell! Lord, please remove this feeling from me – it is not serving me well.

Monday July 29, 2013

I woke up this morning to the most beautiful text message from Warren, my friend and clinical supervisor at STAND. I truly appreciate the friendships that I made during my short time there. It truly helps to have friends who are also counselors, and even more helpful having positive and spiritual people around me right now. He reminded me of the fresh yellow tulips that I kept on my office desk at all times, and how the bright yellow tulips lifted everyone's spirit in that dreary and gray drug treatment center. He said that they symbolized how I bring light to other people's lives. I'm not feeling like a beacon of light at this moment, but the thought is nice and it was great hearing from him.

Today I woke up feeling stiff but better than previous days. I spoke with my brother, Quinn, five times today. We spoke about me doing a segment on the Good Morning America Show. This is overwhelming; am I supposed to be a spokesperson for domestic violence or what? I'm still getting use to all of this media attention. This is not enjoyable for me, but I'm sure that this will become old news very soon. There is a new tragedy every day.

I am so concerned about my lack of physical contact with my children. They are becoming too accustomed to being without me and it's breaking my heart. I feel closer to Chris than before, although I'm not with him daily. We talk on the phone and communicate even more than before. He prays with me and tells me that he loves me every day, but as a counselor, I worry about him inwardly processing and not outwardly expressing his true feelings. I never see him cry or show any emotion, and that concerns me because I know how much he's hurting. When Elon is hurting, everyone knows it because she expresses her feelings at all times, but Chris is very different, which makes me worry about him even more. Lord, please watch over my babies. Please heal their hearts…

Strangely, as ugly as I am, I don't feel depressed today. Speaking out publicly is making me feel empowered and optimistic about the future. I no longer feel totally alone and forgotten. I thank God for my comrades: my mom and my stepdad, Bill, my brother, Machon, LaNese, Jonell, Francis, and Warren. They are all keeping me lifted. It's been three months and one day since he changed my life forever. I will never be the same again. I can only hope that I will be better than before. My mom keeps saying that God is going to restore me and that I will be even more beautiful than before. There are days when her faith must carry us both because this looks so impossible to me. I miss my old face and my old life, but I'm praying that I will have a suitable face and a more abundant life because I have a better appreciation for life. I miss my babies so much, but I'm trying to put my wants and needs aside and allow them to adjust to my altered face and our altered life, in their own way and in their own time. We were so close before, but now I feel like I'm losing my own children. It hurts Elon too much to see me and she's having anxiety so badly that it's causing her stomach problems – she's missing school. This man has cost us so much, and he has no remorse about it. I will not allow myself to be bitter, but I will not stop fighting until justice is served.

Francis sent me yellow tulips today. He is so kind and thoughtful. Like Warren, he also remembered that I kept fresh tulips on my desk at work. I appreciate that he remembered my love for them. They brought me joy on this cloudy day, they reminded me of home and STAND. I thank God for good friends. I am blessed within this mess.

Warren said something powerful today that spoke to me. He said, "Let God's Light shine through your agony so that it may bring you healing and Him glory." I love a Godly man…

Sunday August 4, 2013

It's been three months and one week since that fateful day. Today I am feeling physically, emotionally, and mentally uncomfortable. I have no pain, just overall discomfort. I no longer feel at home in my own skin, a pleasure that I have always enjoyed. The skin on my chest and arms is tight and contracted, and the skin on my face is so tight that it is pulling on my lower eyelids. I waited all this time to see the ocular surgeon to no avail. Her only solution was to patch my lower eyelid, when my primary concern is the function and appearance of both of my eyes. I pray that the plastic surgeons at Emory will have better news next week. I can't imagine having to live this existence for another six months before having surgery. Lord, I need relief and I need it soon. My neck is fused to my face, which makes it difficult to move my head and it makes me look like a freak. There is no way that I'm going in public like this. My body does not feel well enough to travel. I did the Tom Joyner Morning Show on Friday, and my brother said that it had little impact because I sounded too strong; he said that I downplayed my condition too much. He believes that I'm in denial about how bad this is; he could be right. I could not say on a nationally syndicated show that I was completely disfigured. I could not form the words. Denial is the first stage of grief. I'm certain that I'm vacillating back and forth between stage one and stage two, which is anger. Lord knows I'm angry. I'm mad as hell!

It is being suggested that I go national with this story, and going national means showing my face. I think it's too soon and I'm not there yet physically, emotionally, or mentally. I'm already isolated from my children and that is weighing heavily on all of us. Having my burned and disfigured face all over the national news would be devastating for Chris and Elon, and they are my first priority. It's not time; they are not ready. I am not ready. I'm trying really hard not to hate this man, and I find it difficult to say his name out loud. I pray for his empty soul and that he be delivered from evil. That's all that I have to say about that.

Thursday August 15, 2013

I'm sitting in my room at the Holiday Inn in Baltimore waiting for Machon to finish showering so that we can finally go meet the renowned Dr. Robert Spence, Director of the Burn Reconstruction Center at the Good Samaritan Hospital in Baltimore, Maryland. I am hoping that he will give me a good prognosis. I was turned away by several plastic surgeons in Atlanta; the last surgeon said that he could do nothing for me and suggested that I needed a full face transplant. I cried all day for several days after that appointment, but my spirits were lifted when Machon told me about Dr. Spence and the possibility of burn reconstruction in lieu of a face transplant.

Dr. Spence may be my last hope at a normal life. I pray that he will have a kind and optimistic spirit. The previous surgeons broke my heart and crushed my hopes. I pray that this doctor is qualified for my unique needs. I pray that my appearance doesn't disturb him or his staff. I pray that I like him and that he gives me hope. I pray...

Machon and I have not lived together as a couple in six years. I had forgotten that he takes forever to get dressed. Dude, chop chop, let's go, I want my life back! It is so weird being here with him. We were married for 14 years and we have traveled all over the world together. We have been in many hotel rooms together, but this is very different. We are here for a common goal, and here as friends and as parents of Elon and Chris. Our common goal is to get me well enough to go home to them and resume my role as their mother. I know this man must be exhausted, but he hasn't complained. He drove for ten straight hours to get me here. I wish I could have helped him drive, but I'm still as blind as a bat. He has been incredible throughout this ordeal, not just a good father, but he's been an amazing friend to me. He has always been a good person, but this tragedy has made him more unselfish, more forgiving, more kind, and more attentive and gracious.

Hiding myself is taking a toll on me. I am both nervous and optimistic about this appointment. I just want to get past it. I need to meet this brilliant man and hear what he has to say. His opinion will weigh heavily because he specializes in burn reconstruction.

Dr. Spence and Lori walked in and greeted us both. I've been speaking to Lori for several days leading up to this trip so she felt familiar to me. She is not what I imagined – I imagined her blond and much older, but she's a very pretty brunette and I'm guessing that she's just a few years older than me, maybe late 40s. She has a very warm and welcoming personality; I like her very much.

Dr. Spence is taller and more attractive than I had imagined. I would guess that he is about 60 years old based only on him being completely gray, but he has no wrinkles, not even on his hands and neck which are the true signs of a person's age. He is the picture of health. I'd bet a million bucks that he runs at least three miles every day before he comes to work. Not one hair on head is out of order; he is neat and meticulous in appearance. He probably uses some special creams or something because he looks too young to have practiced medicine for 40 years. In any case, he looks nearly flawless. His presence and calm demeanor instantly reassured me that this trip was not in vain. I knew immediately that he would be the surgeon to help me because I could see the compassion in his eyes when he saw how badly I had been burned. I could see his compassion before he ever uttered a word. I searched for the apprehension, the doubt, and the fear that I had seen in the previous surgeon's eyes, but it was not there. All I saw was empathy and a desire to help me. Unlike the previous doctor, he came close to examine me, and he touched me which assured me that he was comfortable in my presence.

There was no need for me to get another opinion. We had already researched him, and we'd already talked to several people at the hospital about his overall skills and personality. I knew all that I needed to know about him. I knew that this process could take years and that I would have a long-term relationship with whomever my surgeon is, so the doctor as a human being was almost as important to me as his level of skill and expertise. Dr. Spence was the one, I had no doubt. He was both humble and confident, which is extremely rare, especially in a skilled surgeon. He was kind, genuine and very direct. He offered me no promises about the future, but he did not turn me away as the other doctors had done. I thank God that he did not turn me away. I appreciated his honesty, I appreciated his compassion, and his bedside manner was incredible. We went back home to Atlanta with hope. My prayers for the right doctor had been answered. I am so grateful to Machon for finding Dr. Spence and for driving me all the way to Baltimore from Atlanta to meet with him. I do not know any other ex-husband that would do that for his ex-wife. I will always love him and I will never forget this. I will always be there for him.

Thursday August 22, 2013

My mood is mixed between despair and exhilaration. I just got off the phone with a mental health counselor from Blue Cross Blue Shield named Regina, and it was a very uplifting and positive conversation. Wow, another angel named Regina. My angel nurse at Emory was named Regina. God sends angels to me every day to help me in this hell. This phone call came just when I needed it. I can see His grace and mercy in the midst of it all. God operates through his people, indeed He does. The Blue Cross Regina reminded me that I am a divine spirit having a human experience. I believe this to my core, and it is my awareness of the temporary nature of things in this life, even my burned and disfigured body--that makes this somehow bearable. She also spoke of the Book of Job in the Bible and how he lost everything and regained it all three times over. I have read the Book of Job many times, but I needed her to remind me of it today. I think of Job on my darkest days and I remind myself that sometimes bad things happen to truly good people, but ultimately we prevail if we continue to trust in God.

Chris and Elon have started back to school. I missed Chris's first day of high school, and Elon's first day of fifth grade a few weeks ago and it broke my heart that I could not be there. I have never missed any "firsts" in my kid's lives. Sigh. They both went to counseling today. They both hate counseling with a passion, and their dad had to drag them there kicking and screaming. I can only hope that he found the right therapist and that they will have a safe forum in which to express themselves. Chris shuts down completely in counseling. I'm glad that he and I communicate well, but I know that he doesn't tell me everything because I am the source of the pain. I just want my kids to be happy and whole again, and to be covered on all sides throughout this ordeal. I feel like scum for creating this situation through my personal decisions. I should have listened to my kids, I should have listened to myself and my intuition. We all screamed, "No!", but I did not listen.

I went to bed feeling blue last night because the process is moving so slowly. The case was reopened, but Drew has still not been charged nor have his name and face been mentioned in the media, so no one knows that he's my abuser, and that concerns me. He is free to come back to hurt me or possibly another woman. My only recourse right now is a temporary restraining order.

I woke up to several loving texts from friends and family. I also talked to my comforter and shadow friend – my "cocoa butter" and as I always, I felt uplifted and inspired. Our conversations are long and meaningful, I get lost within them. We talk about our past, our present, and share dreams about our future. I forget that I am in hell when we talk. I love his spirit, I love the sound of his voice. He is like cocoa butter for my heart and for my soul. He soothes me, he calms me. He loves me and reminds me of a time we were free…he came back to comfort me.

To God be the glory, I am regaining more of my sight. My brother, Quinn surprised me with a laptop today so that I could send emails and handle some of my business while I am recovering. I feel so isolated and alone. I feel forgotten. I think that I will get back on Facebook so that I can have some contact with other people. This isolation is not healthy for my mind, my body, or my soul.

Sunday August 25, 2013

Love really does conquer evil. I am surrounded by love on all sides. It flows through and around me at all times. I could feel an angel there with me on that day as I was sitting in the hallway burning, even in the midst of the evil and chaos. Through God's love, grace, and mercy I will be healed and I will survive evil.

I went face to face with Drew in court on Friday and won a small victory. After hearing our testimonies, a Fulton County judge awarded me with a 12 month protective order against him although he has not yet been charged. Our legal system is very interesting. My volunteer attorney questioned him about the acid attack and the events following it, and then to my surprise, the judge allowed Drew, the man who tried to destroy me, to cross examine me because he did not have an attorney present. To say that this was re-traumatizing is an understatement. This was my first time seeing the face of this man since I saw his image in the bathroom mirror standing behind me, just after he doused me and just before I lost my vision. Seeing him Friday confirmed for me just how evil he truly is. He displayed no emotion and no remorse for completely altering my life. I sat there utterly broken and totally unrecognizable. I looked him directly into his eyes as he questioned me. I searched for some sign of remorse from this man who once said he loved me and wanted to marry me, this man who was once my friend and my lover. I'm not sure what I was expecting, but I saw no evidence of humanity in his eyes. I was hoping for some sign of humanity, but it was not there. He seemed annoyed that we were interrupting his day. He walked smugly out of the courtroom after I was awarded the restraining order which prevents him from coming within 200 yards of me and my kids. He left the court out of a separate exit door and went about his life, and I went back to the isolation of my bedroom in my mother's home.

Sunday September 1, 2013

Today I am not feeling enlightened, uplifted, empowered, or spiritual. I am feeling angry today. I am missing my life, my home, my clients, my daughter, my walks in the park by the lake, my ability to drive, my ability to freely go out in public, my ability to run three miles, my beautiful skin, my attractive face, my laughter and the laughter of my children, my peace and happiness. I am angry at myself for allowing evil into my life. I am angry that my children have to be in counseling and about how this evil act has affected everyone that I love. I am angry that he still walks freely. I am angry that I will never be the same again. I am angry that this happened to me. I have never intentionally hurt anyone in my entire life. I helped people for a living. I have chosen to help those with the least among us, and I have the capacity in my heart to love the entire world. Why me?! I am pissed off!!! Hopefully tomorrow will be a better day.

Thursday September 5, 2013

A local radio personality, Sasha the Diva arranged for me to interview with the top anchor woman in Atlanta, Lisa Rayam of FOX 5 News today at the COX Studio. I am so glad that it is Lisa. My last interview was with Tom Reagan of Channel 2 Action News. He and his crew were very genuine and compassionate. He mentioned that his son had miraculously survived a brain injury last year and I instantly felt more comfortable with him. I connect better with people who have experienced their own tragedy because it makes them more empathetic. Reporters can be pushy and exploitive, but I did not feel that energy with Tom. He was calm and genuine.

I believe that Lisa Rayam is the right person for this next interview because

I am appearing for the first time on TV and I believe that she will be gracious, professional, and empathetic. I have watched her for many years on the news and I read her personal story of tragedy. I am certain than she is the one to properly shed light on this story.

I told my story completely in shadow with Tom back in July, so I'm not certain if the public was impacted by that interview. I was too messed up physically and emotionally to show myself then. But drastic things require drastic measures. My case is moving too slowly and it is time for people to get a better idea of what has been done to me.

My plan is to cover my face with a scarf in this interview today. Elon has only seen me once and it was traumatizing for her, so there is no way that I am showing my entire face. I fear how this might affect my children and my family, but I have prayed about it and it is time.

My mother and I met my brother at the studio and we were slipped in through the private back entrance as if I were celebrities dodging the paparazzi or something. It is actually kind of funny. My face is so disturbing that I have to come in back doors now. This is so unbelievable. The staff at COX were very accommodative as we waited for Lisa to arrive.

She arrived within 10 minutes. She is as beautiful and elegant in person as she is on the news. I liked her immediately and I could instantly see the goodness and the God in her. She was definitely the one. Just as I had guessed, she was kind, caring, compassionate, and empathetic. She was also very genuine and I felt comfortable in her presence. I could not help but feel empathy and concern for her as well because I had read years ago that her husband was murdered in front of her while vacationing. In that moment, I imagined her pain and I silently prayed for her. After introductions and talking for a while, we began the interview that would finally give the public a glimpse of the horror that my family and I had been enduring for months.

The interview was emotional, but very impactful based on the public's response. FOX 5 Atlanta was the first to release Drew's name and face to the public. I have never mentioned his name in the media and I don't plan on doing it. But, his name is public knowledge so I guess the media is free to release it. He has displayed no remorse about what he has done to me. I wonder what his reaction was to seeing himself on the news. I wonder if he will try to hurt me or my family further. Trying to understand the inner workings of the mind of such an evil person is futile, I suppose

Monday September 9, 2013

Lord please put the right words in my mouth so that I may glorify You. Speak through me. I'm headed out in a few minutes to do the Headline News interview. This interview will take my story national, so as much as I hate to walk into the CNN center looking like a freak, it must be done. The producers would prefer that I show my face for this national interview so that it garners the needed national attention, but I am not ready and my children are not ready for my face to be plastered across the country. So, as usual I am cloaked in a scarf and wearing sunglasses. Mom and I arrived at the offices of Headline News, which is located in the CNN Center in downtown Atlanta. I cannot believe that I am in such a public place, in the middle of the day and looking like this. I must really be courageous. This is so difficult for me, but so necessary.

I taped the interview partially in shadow, and then I went home to prepare for my first trip to Baltimore tomorrow.

Wednesday September 11, 2013

Mom and I arrived safely in Baltimore yesterday. It was my first time flying like this and of course I got a lot of stares in the airport. I believe that it makes my mom more uncomfortable than me, and I hate seeing the look in her eyes when strangers gawk at me, but she remains silent and so do I. This is our life right now, and this trip is the beginning of my reconstruction process, the beginning of my new life, and thus it is worth the stares of few strangers. I must say that we Tucker girls are some bad ass women. My grace and resilience is hereditary; I got it from my mama, and she got it from her mama. We are "Steel Magnolias" – soft as a flower, yet tough as steel.

Today is the 12th anniversary of 9-11, and I am having my first facial surgery. This surgery is merely for functionality. It is necessary to correct my eyelids and improve my vision, but whose brilliant idea was it to schedule my surgery on one of the worst days in American history?! This cannot be a good omen, yet here I go being courageous again. Inside I am screaming – I am terrified. I have had six surgeries thus far, but those were done at the Grady Burn Unit while I was in a coma. I am fully aware of this surgery, and before a few months ago, I had only been in the hospital to have my babies. I do not like hospitals; they freak me out, but I guess I had better get accustomed to them because I have many years of surgeries to come. The thought of having my entire face taken off and put back on is frightening to me, and I am suddenly filled with so much fear and so much anger. I have been suppressing it as much as I could, but in this moment I truly despise Andrew Fordham Jr. and I hope that he rots in hell.

Surgery # 7 Dr. Spence repaired both of my lower eyelids by grafting skin from my stomach. I should be able to see out of my left eye after this surgery. He also repaired my right arm so that I can fully extend it, since it was contracted in a 90 degree angle when I woke up from the coma. He also inserted two tissue expanders to each side of my stomach so that we can harvest to skin to prepare me for my remaining surgeries. For the next year, in addition to being burned and crazy looking, due to the tissue expanders I will also have an increasingly inflated stomach, which will make me look pregnant. Burned and pregnant-looking...great. Hell certainly cannot be any worse than this. Kick rocks Fordham...you suck.

Anyway, my eyelids are bandaged closed, so for the ten days while in recovery here, I be will totally dependent upon my mom and only able to listen to music. I am in pain, I am depressed, but I have survived surgery #7 and hopefully I will look a little better so that I can see the kids when I get back. My eyes are what disturbed Elon the most so I am hoping that this will help. This sucks, it really does. I'm so glad that I have LaNese and my mom here. LaNese and I have been best friends since the ninth grade. She has been heaven sent. She was there with mom while I went through surgery, and she has made sure that we have everything that we need while I'm here recovering. She is yet another yellow tulip on the horrible and cloudy day. It is not by happenstance that my best friend in the entire world just happens to live near the city where all of my surgeries will be performed. I see You, God, I see You. Ten more days of recovery in this hotel room and then we can fly home.

Tuesday September 17, 2013

I'm so thankful that I chose to marry and have children with Machon. I met him when I was 19 years old. He walked up to me and said, "Don't be offended, but you look just like this fraternity brother of mine at the University of Georgia." I wasn't sure if I should be offended or not, but I laughed out loud because I knew instantly that he was talking about my brother, Quinn. My brother and I are four years apart, but we look like twins. Machon showed interest in me throughout college, but he was two years older, so he graduated prior to me and moved away to take a job in Jacksonville, Florida.

Over the years we would cross paths because he and my brother were not just fraternity brothers, but very close friends as well. Machon is the one who introduced my brother to his first wife, so we were both at their wedding. However, we still never connected. It wasn't until I was invited by his roommates Jason and Reginald to his 25th birthday party that we began to truly connect. I saw him in his element. He was genuine and charismatic, and he had the most amazing smile. He still has one of the best smiles on the planet. He said that he had always been attracted to me, but I was always dating someone else so he did not pursue me. After seeing him that night we began to speak on the phone often, and we began to date as I was just starting my corporate career. I was 23 years old and my life was finally falling into place. I had been doing odd jobs since college and I was on the rebound from my last relationship. I felt scattered, as if four years of college had been a total waste of my time and money, but I began to pray and be deliberate in my requests to God. Within a month's time, I rededicated my life to God, I joined a new church, I started my new job with Lockheed Martin, and I was now dating this really amazing guy. I liked Machon a lot; being with him felt natural to me.

We became inseparable. We dated for two years and I fell in love with both him and his entire family. We spent every Sunday at his aunt Gail's house and I became a part of their family. Machon bought his first home and then I bought a little starter home, but we spent all of our time together. We dated for two years, and then he asked me to marry him on February 13, 1996. He proposed to me the day before Valentine's Day so that I could go to work on the next day and flash my new ring on the actual holiday. Thinking back, that was not the kind of ring that you boast about. The diamond in my engagement ring was so tiny that you needed a search party to find it. Neither of us made a lot of money at that time. I didn't care how big the ring was, I was just excited to be getting married. I had no doubt that he was the right one for me at that time. Machon and I just fit; we never argued about anything. We were engaged for a few months and got married later that year on November 23, 1996. It was the most beautiful fall day. I looked and felt beautiful. We had a large wedding with over 300 guests, 10 bridesmaids and 10 groomsmen. My father walked me down the aisle and seemed so proud of me in that moment. I will never forget the look on Machon's face as I walked down the aisle. He looked at me with so much adoration, I felt as if I was the most loved and the most beautiful woman I the world.

We were so happy in the beginning of our marriage. We were spontaneous and fun and we absolutely adored each other. Before the kids were born, sometimes we would hop in the car and just drive without knowing where we were headed. We would we stop and stay wherever the road led us. We made no reservations, we made no elaborate vacation plans, we just enjoyed each other's company and we knew that as long as we were together, all would be well. I didn't just love Machon back then, I truly liked him as a person and I was the happiest when I was in his presence. He was solid and dependable. He made me laugh out loud. After three years of marriage, Chris was born and we were both elated. We were truly a family. He began his career in pharmaceutical sales and my real estate career was blossoming. I absolutely loved the freedom and the money. This was the best time in our marriage, we were so happy.

Two years passed and we learned that we were pregnant with our second baby. I was ecstatic to find out that it was a baby girl. I envisioned dressing her like a little doll and she and I having matching outfits. I worked as a real estate agent throughout my pregnancy, and everything seemed normal.

We named her Kayla and she was the most beautiful baby. She weighed 8.2 lbs and had a head of thick, curly black hair. She looked like my grandmother, Dorothy. We brought her home to the dream house we had built the prior year and our family was now complete. Our life was perfect. We had a boy and a girl, we lived in a beautiful home, we had plenty of money, and we truly loved each other. We had an enviable life. It was more than either of us had ever planned or imagined. But, it all changed on a sunny Saturday morning in October.

Kayla's heart stopped and so did ours. She passed away from congenital heart failure on October 27, 2001 and our marriage was never the same again. Our hearts were broken. Apart of me died that day. We retreated to our separate corners and we never fully recovered. Machon and I separated in 2008 and later divorced in 2010. In spite of everything, I have absolutely no regrets about the years that I spent as his wife. I was the happiest that I have ever been in my life. Our divorce was messy and I could have handled it so much better. I should have fought harder for our marriage, but I was so heartbroken over Kayla and so unhappy in general. We resented each other for not being able to hold our family together, so we said the most hateful things to each other. I wish that I had the emotional fortitude then that I have now. I pray for his happiness. I hope that he has truly forgiven me. I hope that he finds someone to love him as much as I did. I'm so grateful that my kids have a loving and caring father to care for them in my absence. I'm so grateful for those years of bliss.

Thursday September 19, 2013

I have never been a vain person. I grew up in southwest Atlanta surrounded by beautiful brown people in all shapes and sizes, and thus I perceived beauty as being normal and relative. I considered myself to be attractive but average, I suppose. Beauty was simply not my priority; I focused mostly on being a kind person. But now that my appearance has changed so drastically, I find myself looking at previous photos of myself as if I'm looking at another person. I can now say with confidence that I was one of those pretty girls. I had a beautiful face with a great smile. I had high cheek bones, dimples and freckles. I truly miss being pretty. I know that beauty is within, but being beautiful both inside and out was nice and I want that back. Why did he have to destroy my face? The inhumanity is what breaks my heart…

Saturday September 21, 2013

Hello, my name is Christy, and I am a serial monogamist. I have been in relationships since I was 12 years old. I've only been in few relationships, including a 14 year marriage; but they were all long and deep, and I thought that I was in love each time. Being a Leo woman is both a curse and a blessing. Leos are known to love hard and long, and we love being in love. We are generous with our time, with our hearts, and with our money. I will love you, your mama, and your dog. It took me all this time to realize that with each relationship, I was subconsciously searching for my father, and thus every relationship was doomed from the start because no man can replace the love that a girl should receive from her father. As a result of this tragedy, I am healed in this area because my daddy has been here for me. He has actually been there all along.

Sunday September 22, 2013

My greatest challenge right now is learning to be happy within this hell. For most of my life, I've walked around with this feeling of discontentment. No matter how much money I made or how much success I achieved, I still wasn't truly happy with myself. I was never enough. It took many years, but after Machon and I divorced, I began to explore myself and to seek happiness diligently. The first key to finding happiness is discovering what makes you happy. What makes me happy is quiet time with God, fresh yellow tulips or sunflowers, the beach at sunrise and sunset, the look on Chris's face when he scores in baseball and basketball, the look on Elon's face when she scores a goal or lands a backhand spring in gymnastics. Happiness is witnessing my kids learning something new, movie nights, buffets with crab legs, a good book, a great conversation with a funny and intelligent person, happy and positive people, 50% off shoe sales, great sex, my clients when they are clean and sober and rebuilding their lives, a clean and well decorated home, a long walk by the lake, finishing something difficult, a healthy and loving relationship, my babies' first everything, and lately, since I can't see them daily, the mere sound of my kids' voices over the phone sends me to the moon with joy. I have yet to see Elon again and I miss her so much.

It is amazing how we receive knowledge just when we need it the most. I was just watching Oprah's Life Class, and I had another lightbulb moment. She was interviewing author and public speaker, Brene' Brown on the subject of vulnerability. Lately I have been struggling to find my role in this new life that was forced upon me. I have now been labeled by the world as Courageous Christy – they even have T-shirts now – but I don't feel courageous or strong at all most days. I am afraid of the unknown. I am terrified of living this way for the rest of my life. Today Brene' said something that gave me peace. She gave me permission to be both courageous and afraid at the same time because courage is not the absence of fear, but the ability to operate in spite of it, and that is what I am doing by speaking up and fighting back. I am fighting for me, for my children, and for every person who did not live to tell their story. I have no choice in this matter, God is propelling me forward. In spite of my scars, I will continue to speak out in the media. I will continue to fight back. I have fear, but fear does not have me.

Monday September 23, 2013

I spoke with my cocoa butter friend this morning. We speak nearly every day now and I am becoming increasingly more dependent upon him for comfort. I look forward to his calls each day because he is my only escape. As much as talking to the kids brings me joy, it also makes me sad and it makes me feel guilty because I cannot be with them. I see Chris often, but Elon is still not ready to be around me daily. This is a lot for a 10-year old girl…hell, this is a lot for me.

Today I shared with my cocoa butter friend how much I miss being a beautiful and sexy woman. I have lost everything that makes me look and feel like a woman, except my curvaceous body. Thank God you can't burn curves. I have no feminine features to my face; in fact, I really don't have a face at all. Every inch of my face is burned to the third degree. It is hard to express in writing how bad this truly is. I have no choice but to take pictures of this hideous process. As much as I hate to see myself on camera, something within me tells me that I will be glad that I have a record of just how awful this is. My hope is that one day I will have improved so much that looking back on this time won't hurt so much. I can only pray that God performs the supernatural miracle that mom speaks of daily. I want so desperately to be attractive again. Dr. Spence has made it clear that I will never look like a normal person, but I am still hoping for the best that is possible. I am still believing in the God of miracles. I now have more of my vision back, so anything is possible.

Tuesday September 24, 2013

Sandi Rivers called this morning to check on me and to give me an update. I really like this woman, and I can feel her sincerity. She said that there was still no news of a grand jury date and still no progress in the case. She asked me several questions about the events leading up to the day that Drew attacked me and I shared with her every detail, down to the color of the boxers that he was wearing when he attacked me. Sandi seems to truly believe me, but I could hear it in her voice that she was having challenges taking this case to the grand jury. She said that she was fighting an uphill battle because the Henry County Police Department had not done an initial investigation. I told Sandi not to worry because the truth would be revealed and all that I required was that she do her best and not give up on this case. She made me no promises as usual, but she assured me that she would do her job as ADA and seek the prosecution of Fordham. She asked once again if I was certain that I was strong enough to endure this process and possibly a lengthy criminal trial. I replied, "What choice do I have Sandi? If someone threw acid in your face, would you just lay down without a fight?" She replied back to me, "No Christy I would not. Let's move forward."

After my call with Sandi, the hearts and minds of my children are weighing more heavily on me than normal. I wonder if people consider that when they hurt a mother, they hurt her innocent children as well. Elon is taking this the hardest because her beauty and identity are directly tied to mine because she is my little girl, and she has always been proud of looking like her pretty mommy. I would imagine that within her young mind, she poses the question, "Who do I look like now?" I am a divorced mom so my son considered himself to be the man of the house and my protector, and he is now carrying unwarranted guilt and warranted heartache over not being there to protect me. This is too much evil for me to process, so I can only imagine how hard it is for my children, who have been surrounded by love their entire lives. I know that I will forgive this man for what he has done to me, but it may take until the next lifetime for me to forgive him for the pain that he has caused my babies. I have seen Chris often, but I have only seen Elon once in four months because she was traumatized the first time that she saw me. Through counseling, we are working our way back to each other.

Machon, his mom, Connie, and his aunt, Gail have been my saving grace, but I am their mother and it is my job to nurture them. I am missing so much of their lives right now and it is breaking my heart. We will never be able to recover this time apart. I did everything in my power to create lasting memories for Chris and Elon as they were younger. I wanted them to be able to look back on their childhood fondly and with joy. I wanted them to remember our times on the beach. I wanted them to remember that they had parents that loved and wanted them. I wanted them to have a better childhood than I had, but I fear now that this horrible thing will be their prevailing childhood memory, and the thought of it breaks my heart and overwhelms me with guilt and shame and frustration, and with so much disdain for Drew that I can hardly contain myself. In the process of forgiving him, I hope that I can forgive me.

It is sometimes hard to see one's own picture from inside one's own frame. I am a critically thinking, confident, strong, well-educated, well-loved, professional counselor; yet I could not see my own picture clearly until it was too late. My son Chris is highly intuitive and spiritual, and I have always known that he can see and feel the spirits of other people. He told me one month before the attack that whenever Drew was around a siren went off inside of him and he felt danger. He said it with so much sincerity that I had to believe him, and his words resonated within me because I too had felt that same siren, that same warning sign signaling me to walk away. I honored Chris' words by promising him that he would not have to be around Drew again, and that I would never marry him. After this conversation with Chris, I started backing away from Drew. I did not break up with him abruptly because his father was dying from cancer, and I didn't feel that it was the compassionate thing to do. In spite of everything, I still had this since of loyalty to him and a concern for his well-being. I also did not believe that I was in imminent danger because we were getting along well during that time. Children have a sixth sense that adults dismiss as we gain more logic. It is important to listen to them when they speak. God may be speaking through them; I know that He was in my case. I should not have backed away – I should have run away immediately.

Wednesday September 25, 2013

Yesterday was a day of cleansing. I cried from sun up until sun down. I cried so much that my head hurt and my cheeks burned from the tears. I really was not that sad, I just felt like crying for no particular reason, so I let it flow. Today, I'm all cried out and all I can say is "I surrender." This battle is not mine, Lord, it is Yours. Let Your will be done in my life. I'm simply not brilliant enough, not courageous enough, nor am I strong enough to carry this heavy load. Where ever You want me to go, I will go. Whatever you want me to say, I will say; and whatever You want me to endure, I will endure. My plan obviously wasn't working, so I'm following Yours now and operating by faith and not by sight. There is nowhere for me to go from here but up and forward. I surrender…

Thursday September 26, 2013

Inger Jackson Garnett, an old friend from middle school sent me this message on Facebook today and it blessed my soul:

My Dearest Christy, Let me begin this note by first offering you my repentance. Since you shared your story in July, God has put you on my heart to pray and intercede for you and also to send this note of encouragement--because of my own concerns about how it would be perceived and my own pride, I have been disobedient. So let me sincerely apologize to you for being disobedient and not following God's lead. I know that as I type this note to you, you are going through some life challenges. But I come to you with a breath of encouragement to let you know that God loves you so much! I am sure deep in your heart you know that, but let me share with you what He has put on my heart in order to show you just how intimately He is concerned with every fiber of your being. Although we do not know each other well and only met each other in middle school, from the time you shared your journey, God has put a burning urgency in my heart to pray, intercede and stand in the gap for you. Sometimes, I couldn't understand why at 2am, 3am, and 4am you would be on my mind and in my heart. But you were…again with a burning need to pray and lift you up in prayer. I am sure I am not the only one. Please know that God loves you so much that He is driving many people that you may know and may not know to go to the throne daily for you and your family. He also loves you so much that what I write to you today it is strictly as God puts on my heart and I pray the angels have prepared your heart to hear the voice of the Lord. God has sent this note to reassure you that what Satan meant for evil, God will make it for your good. In the Word of God, the Lord says to Simon Peter "Simon, behold, Satan hath desired to have you, that he may sift you as wheat. But I (Jesus) have prayed for thee, that thy faith fail not and when thou art converted, strengthen thy brethren." Yes, Christy, Satan came to steal, kill, and destroy you and what is yours, but know that it is not just your friends and others that God is pressing to intercede for you, but Jesus himself is praying for you daily. He is praying that your faith will not fail you, and because you are His…it will not! Years ago while serving in the Navy as a Medical Service Corp officer, I too was in an abusive relationship. And as I moved on and was healed from the ordeal, I could look back and see all of the signs that were there. I was away from my family and friends in the military where I did not know anyone, so I leaned on this man for both mental and emotional support. And he recognized this and tried to isolate me further. He would talk about me being too close with my mom and my family. He would put down my education, my background, my appearance, and my friends in a subtle manner. He would not say it directly, but he made comments that slowly tore away my self-esteem and made me more dependent on him and his approval. He would also blame his issues, his infidelity and even his anger on me. When I finally started to back away…the accusations, the put downs, and the aggression increased. And because he was enlisted in the military and I was an officer, and we were prohibited from seeing each other by military law, he also used that too to his advantage. So it left me with lots of emotional, mental and some physical scars in an isolated world. Although my ending in this relationship did not bear the physical scars that you have today. I did try to take my life to deal with my emotional scars. But Christy, I am writing to you to say But God! But God healed, restored and turned my life around and as His word says He gave me beauty for ashes. I am writing to reassure you that He is going to do the same for you and more. renew your life-it will be greater than before! As I said, He is going to give you beauty for ashes…in your health, in your family, in your finances and also in the justice that you seek. But in all these areas, I decree to you to "be still and know that He is God." Love you with the love of the Lord. Your Sister, Your Friend Inger.

Once again, I see You, Lord. I see You working through Your people. I haven't seen Inger Jackson in over 30 years, but I feel strangely connected to her now. I receive messages daily now from both friends and strangers, but this one was different. Her message was filled with hope and sincerity – it was filled with God. It could not have been easy for her to reveal the details of her abusive relationship when we have not communicated since eighth grade. Her message touched me, it is what I needed on this particular day. Something in my spirit tells me that Inger and I will be life-long friends.

Saturday September 28, 2013

As I rise to face this lovely and breezy fall day; I am remembering my joy. It was five months ago today that my life changed forever. Five months ago I was the happiest that I had ever been in my life. As I said, I had made it through the storm of divorce. I had the least amount of money I have ever had and I lived in the smallest house I have ever owned. Still, I had found peace and joy in little things, in simple things. I was on a natural high that day. Then, within the blink of an eye, he doused my dreams, my hopes, my career, my beauty, and my identity. He tried to put out the beaming light inside of me; I guess it was too bright for him in the midst of his darkness. He succeeded temporarily – I have lost a lot and my light is dimmer now, but as my wonderful friend and colleague Francis said to me today, "Christy, there are over 100 types of light bulbs, you can replace that dimmed light...now get up and live!" Thank you my friend, I think that I will do just that.

Even in the midst of chaos and confusion, peace is attainable and happiness is a choice. I don't want to just survive, I want to live a life that is abundant and full of joy. Happiness is a choice, and I have made my choice.

Sunday September 29, 2013

I'm still not with my kids and it's tearing away at my soul. My light was a bit dim again today because I'm so uncomfortable, I feel so isolated and alone, and I miss Chris and Elon so much. Still, I did not host a pity party. I did not cry – instead I got up and thanked God for this five months of life. I showered and got dressed as cute as possible, in spite of my funny looking face. I polished my toes hot pink, I listened to gospel music, I wrote both of my babies love letters and mailed them. Later, I went to the mall and the movies with my mom and Bill for the first time since before. This was monumental; I have not had any outside entertainment in five months, but I wanted to see the movie "Baggage Claim," so I put on my camouflage to cover my face. I put on my "big girl panties" and my Courageous Christy Cape, and I went out to the movies. I got a few stares from people as usual, but they will be okay, and so will I. The movie was just what I needed. It was actually better than I had expected. It was funny, cute, and romantic. I needed a good laugh and I got it. Mom, Bill, and I all needed a good laugh. Like music, humor is medicine for the soul. I am learning to take it day by day, knowing that one day this will be a distant memory, and when I make it to the other side of this storm and I am restored; everyone will know that God did this miraculous work in my life. I am so excited about Him getting the glory. Today was a pretty good day. I am thankful for even brief moments of joy.

Monday September 30, 2013

I have experienced more mental, emotional, and physical pain in the past five months than some people experience in a life time. I believe that pain truly births our talents and our goals. It is often the catalyst for change. When we are too comfortable, we remain stagnant and do not grow. I have emerged from every trial and tragedy in my life-wiser, stronger, and more compassionate; I grew. This is my greatest trial thus far, so I am expecting the greatest amount of growth.

Tuesday October 1, 2013

I am the most peaceful within my dreams. I've been having this recurring dream for the past few weeks. In the dream, I am looking in the mirror to access my scars, but as hard as I try, I cannot see any burns or disfigurement. In the dream, I know what has happened to me and that I have been severely burned. I squint and rub my eyes, trying hard to see the scars. But the only reflection that I can see in the mirror is the freckled and dimpled face of the original me, before the attack. In this dream I can only see myself the way that I have always been. Then I wake up and look in the mirror excitedly, as if none of the past few months have happened because the dream seemed so real, but there she is, the current me, and I become dismal. I shed a few tears and then I rise to face another day; believing that one day I will again be content with the reflection of me that I see, praying that one day I will again see me.

This extended time alone is breeding a great deal of self-awareness. We often focus more on who others are, what they want and need, and what they think of us, and we focus less on what we think of ourselves. It is important to know who we truly are, otherwise we will always be operating on other's agendas and beliefs about us. I am still evolving, but I know who I am right now. I am spirit personified, I am complex in all areas. I am as naughty as I am nice. I am as classy as I am ghetto. I can lead and follow with equal agility. I am both strong and vulnerable. I am a skilled listener, but I want to be heard as well. I am as comfy in high-heeled shoes as I am in sneakers. I am both sinner and saint. I am an intellectual, but I prefer simple concepts. I either love you or I am totally indifferent to you; there is no in between with me, and I will never hate you because it takes too much energy. I am impatient, disorganized, a procrastinator, and seriously flawed and imperfect. But I am kind, authentic, and positive. I have made some bad decisions, but my intentions are typically good. I trust God even when things are horrible and even when it makes no sense to trust Him because who but God could have brought me through all of that other stuff? There are only two things in life that we can control: #1 Our behavior and #2 How we choose to feel about ourselves. That is all, nothing else. We cannot control others or their behavior. We cannot control sickness or death, or our jobs, or anything else in life. We can only control us. We can only change ourselves.

I have called the Assistant District Attorney, Sandi Rivers every week since we first met. She has been very gracious, but also very direct about my case. She is still working towards a grand jury indictment, but she has no idea when or if it will happen. I am growing weary of our justice system. The longer that I am away from my children, as Drew goes about his life and is able to raise his children, the more weary I become. He should not be free. I am in prison…and he walks free.

October is National Domestic Violence Month. Never in a million years could I have imagined that I would be a victim of domestic violence. But what woman would ever imagine this for herself? I do not fit the statistics. I am secure, I have close family ties, and I am a trained counselor. I was not in a typical cycle of abuse but there were warning signs that I did not act upon quickly enough like jealousy, possessiveness, and controlling behavior. I truly did not believe that I was in eminent danger. This was a planned assault, there was no slip and fall, no clogged drain, and no need for sulfuric acid in my home. I do not speak about my case often or even mention his name because it generates so much negative energy for me. I know that this was intentional and I am certain of that. I will not stop fighting for justice because another person's life may be in danger, and because it is just the right thing to do. My story finally airs on Headline News within the week. It will be featured in the *Atlanta Journal and Constitution* newspaper this week, and in *JET* magazine on October 14th, I believe. I am a private person and I do not like being a victim or known as the woman who was attacked with sulfuric acid; this is not a good look for me. But it happened, it was wrong and it is what it is. I am a survivor of domestic violence.

Thursday October 3, 2013

I am not feeling it today. I am feeling blah, but I am so glad that my kids are out of school and going away for a few days. They need some fun in the sun. I will likely be on the front page of the AJC newspaper tomorrow, and then likely on Headline News next week. I am glad that they will be far away from this foolishness. They will be in the place where kids can be kids. Machon is taking them to Disney World, and I only wish that I could be there with them. I miss being home so much. I have not slept in my own bed in six months.

Just as I was feeling sorry for myself, my cell phone rang and his name came across the display. Just seeing his name instantly changed my mood. He always calls when I need him the most. He is indeed my cocoa butter. At times speaking with him is both bitter and sweet because all we will ever have is our phone conversations. He is such a beautiful man inside and out, but I will never allow him to see me this way. I don't ever want to see the pain in his eyes from looking at me this way. I want him to always remember me as his beautiful CJ. It already destroys me to see the pain in Machon's eyes, in the kids' eyes, and in my family's. I cannot carry the pain of another person who loves me. I still have not shown my face in the media, yet he says that he already knows what I look like. He says that his spirit allows him to see me as I am, and he will accept me in any state. He said that I could be missing my head and he would still love me. We laughed and talked for two hours without a pause. I needed him more than ever today. I needed to escape this hell for just a little while.

Friday October 4, 2013

This poem has been in my head all day. I learned it by memory when I was in Mrs. Smith's 7th grade class. She was the meanest teacher in the world, but she was the first person to recognize the poet trapped inside of me. I did not truly understand this poem until I was one and twenty, and now that I am three and forty, it speaks volumes.

When I Was One-and-Twenty by A. E. Housman

When I was one-and-twenty...
I heard a wise man say,
"Give crowns and pounds and guineas
But not your heart away;
Give pearls away and rubies
But keep your fancy free."
But I was one-and-twenty,
No use to talk to me.

When I was one-and-twenty
I heard him say again,
"The heart out of the bosom
Was never given in vain;
'Tis paid with sighs a plenty
And sold for endless rue."
And I am two-and-twenty,
And oh, 'tis true, 'tis true.

Sunday October 6, 2013

I have been in a quiet and introspective mood for the past few days and I have not felt much like talking. I am feeling tired and weary. It is impossible to be strong every day. Today would have been our daughter Kayla's 12th birthday. I still miss her so much but the throbbing pain in my heart is no longer there and I thank God for that. I walked around with a hole in my heart for many years after her death. Our marriage was never the same after she passed. We were both heart broken and instead of comforting each other, we each retreated and became distant from one another.

She smiled at me for the first and last time, then she closed her eyes and died right in front of me. Apart of me died with her on that sunny Saturday morning. Every year I think that I have gotten beyond that loss, but I have come to realize that some things in life are not meant to get "over"; you just get "through" them. The loss of a child or a parent is one of those things. Some souls come to this life solely for the edification of others. They live and they die so that those who experience them may grow and develop. I believe that my daughter Kayla was one of those souls. She lived for only three weeks but her short life and death transformed me into the woman that I am today. Before her death, I did not know authentic pain. I had compassion and I could imagine how others felt, but I truly did not know until I experienced it for myself. After her death, I stopped just existing and I began to truly live. I held Chris, who was 2 years old at the time even tighter than before and I loved him even more intensely. My heart expanded, my level of empathy and compassion increased, and I became wiser and stronger. I learned that I could lose anything and anyone in this life and still survive it because everything and everyone, including my precious children, are just on loan from God. Everything belongs to Him, the Creator of life. Everything in this life is temporary, and if I can imagine an end to it then I can survive it. I am honored that she chose an imperfect woman like me to be her mother.

I planned just about everything in my life. I designed our dream home, which was a big four sided brick house with stone accents. It had a circular driveway with the fountain in the middle that I had always dreamt of. I had a husband, two kids and a white poodle named Sam. I planned everything but the death of my baby girl. Her death was the game changer that shattered our perfect little life of oblivion. We lived in oblivion, we were on autopilot. We were focused on things and people that did not matter just as a lot of people do, but they do not realize it until their world is shattered like ours.

On the day that Kayla died, I thanked God in advance for the future day when thoughts of her would bring me more joy than pain. That day has finally come, and I am now thanking Him in advance for that future day when this current pain is no more. I know that it will come...

Thursday October 10, 2013

My story just aired on Headline News. It airs again between 6 and 7 pm. I figured out about a week after awakening from the coma that what happened to me is not just about me, and it was then that I began to fight back. My body is too weak to physically fight, so I am doing what I can; I am talking and writing.

Friday October 11, 2013

"Now faith is the substance of things hoped for, the evidence of things not seen." Hebrews 11:1

Elon said to me two years ago "Mommy, I want to believe in God, but how can I be certain that He is real if I cannot see, touch, hear, or feel Him?" I said, "Don't force it baby, over time things will happen in your life that will be so big that you will know that man alone could not have done that, and you will know God through His work, and with each small miracle, your faith will increase. Last week, I said to her "Babe, this is one of those big things that I spoke of. I am hurt badly and when God heals me, you will know that He is real." She replied, "It has already happened mommy, I prayed to God both night and day that you would live and come home, and when you woke up and left the hospital, I knew that God had done that because I asked Him to. I know that God is real!" Needless to say, I was all smiles. My work is done here. Her name is Elon, which means spirited, self-assured, and strong. She is only 10 and she is all these things and more. She is a walking and breathing miracle.

Sunday October 13, 2013

Happiness occurs for me when there is a unique balance and an alignment of the four parts of "Self": spiritual, emotional, mental, and physical. Happiness is a state of being. It should not be dependent upon your finances, relationship status, etc. Five months ago, I had achieved happiness because I was practicing the art of balance every day. I catered to the four parts of myself daily, and it transferred into most of my relationships, into my work as a counselor, and most importantly, into my role as a mother. Happiness can be contagious, but the exception is when you are associating with evil and miserable people. They are annoyed by happy people. I achieved balance by meditating, praying, and reading my Bible (spiritual), by loving and interacting with my family and friends, crying when needed and laughing as much as possible (emotional), by doing introspective work on myself, going to therapy, studying my clients, reading, and talking to my colleagues (mental), and lastly by exercising and eating as healthy as possible (physical). Today happiness is more of a challenge because getting that balance is more of a challenge. My spiritual self is heightened because I spend so much time alone with God. However, my mental self is not on par because I am ever concerned about my life is general. My physical self is way off course because I am uncomfortable every second of the day, and I am heartbroken and angry so my emotional self is seriously lacking as well. Nevertheless, I truly believe that if I can somehow find happiness in this valley, then everything in life after this will be a cake walk. I am working on getting back to that happy place...

Monday October 14, 2013

I am good at identifying whatever I am feeling at any moment and honoring that feeling by giving it a name (sad, angry, happy, confused, etc.), but today I have no name for this feeling. I am feeling a way, and I don't know what that way is. October is not my favorite month. Kayla was born on October 6th, she died on October 27th, and we buried her on October 31st, Halloween. Maybe November will be a better month...

Thursday October 17, 2013

I'm blessed to have a praying mother. I have witnessed many miracles in my life, and several in the past five months. For the first few months of my injury I was blind due to the chemical getting into my eyes. The doctors told my family that I would have vision problems for the rest of my life. My mom said, "The devil is a liar...not my daughter...she will be healed completely, burns, vision and all...I claim it Jesus' name." My mom went into her closet and she prayed. I went to the eye specialist a month ago and my vision had improved drastically. My question was, will I be able to drive my kids to school again? The doctor said, "At the rate you are going, you will drive anywhere you want." I went back again today, and the doctor tested my eyes again and said, "This is unbelievable. You have 20/30 vision in your left eye and although your cornea has been damaged, your right eye is improving as well." I used reading glasses and didn't have 20/30 vision before this happened to me. Eyes typically do not get better; they get worse with age. I am claiming this as another one of many miracles to come. This is how faith increases; this is how God works. I am still in a bad way, but if

God can heal my eyes, then he can heal these burns and make me new. I am expecting a supernatural miracle, the kind in which God specializes.

Saturday October 19, 2013

Music is soothing my soul today. There is so much power in a song. I have been transported back in time by melody. The song "Firecracker" took me way back to a time when I played kick ball and played hide and go seek. It took me back to a time when I practically lived at Greenbriar Skating Rink, caught lightening bugs, sucked honey suckles, and had my first kiss. With the song, "Always" by Pebbles, I re-visited the reverie of my first love, my high school days, the beginning of my lifelong friendships, and the onset womanhood, a time when I felt truly free and life was still a mystery to me. Chaka Khan's version of "My Funny Valentine" is one of my favorite songs and it took me back to my wedding day when I was 26 and fine as wine, and I felt beautiful and loved. I still had that twinkle in my eye, and so much of life was still ahead of me. Now here I am and India Arie has reminded me that "I am not the skin on the outside, I am divinity defined. I am light." Her music also allowed me to visualize the unconditional love that I am receiving as "Cocoa Butter" to my heart. Love is healing me. Lastly, Isacc Caree brought me back to the "now" and reminded me that "No matter what I'm going through, I gotta do my dance, I gotta praise God anyway, right in the middle of it." I love music, because it is yet another survival tool.

Sunday October 20, 2013

I need an owner's manual for this stuff. There is nothing in any parenting book or guide about what to do when some nut throws sulfuric acid in your face, changes your entire appearance and life, and traumatizes your children. How do you explain this type of evil to a child? I am a counselor, but this is a lot for me because it's me. This is bearable most of the time until I see my kids and I see the hurt in their eyes. This really pisses me off! I was doing my praise dance earlier today because I was anticipating seeing them, but I don't feel like dancing right now. No child should have to go through this. People get sick and die every day, but the way this happened to me is some bull. I am on a roller coaster of emotions. I am headed down the curve right now, so hopefully I will be back on an upswing tomorrow.

Monday October 21, 2013

I am on an endless pursuit of wisdom and understanding. I am diligently seeking God and I am finding Him. I am evolving at the speed of light. I am trying desperately to get the lessons during this season so that I don't have to repeat this type of test in this lifetime or the next. The tests keep coming until we truly learn the lessons. The tests are rarely fair and some people have far more challenging tests than others. But if you are strong enough to endure the test, you will become closer to God's brilliant light. You will become less human and more divine. I will pass this test because it was designed for me to pass. I am well. I am healed. I am at peace. I am free. I am, I am, I am...

Tuesday October 22, 2013

My days are up and down. I am still burned and disfigured. I am still living at my mom's house away from the kids, and I am still fighting depression with all that I have in me. I was feeling especially courageous today, so for the first time I accepted my mom's invite to go grocery shopping and I ventured out to Super Walmart during rush hour. Once again, I put on my head gear to cover my funny looking face, I held my head high and I walked into the store. Most people are typically so caught up in themselves that they don't even notice me. But the little kids, they notice every dang thing. This one little boy stood and stared at me in disbelief for more than 5 minutes. I wanted to say BOOOOOOOOOO to really freak him out but I did not...lol. Prior to being burned I got stares because I had a big booty and a beaming smile, but now it is because I am burned beyond belief. This is so crazy. Years ago I taught my kids how to treat disabled people. I said do not stare, but acknowledge their presence and smile, and do not pity them, but be proud of them because it takes a courageous soul to live their existence. Lastly, we should pray for them right there in that moment. Both of my children have always done exactly that, and they have more empathy and compassion than some adults. The only thing I did not prepare them for was what if the person that is physically different is me, the person that they count on to take care of them? I can only hope that this experience will not only make me the warrior woman that God wants me to be, but that it develops my kids into two incredible and purpose driven human beings. I believe that it will...

Wednesday October 23, 2013

Transparency is therapy for me right now; it is why I am being so uncharacteristically open about my life. I feel as though I have been stripped of almost everything, so how much more can anyone do to hurt me? Also, I believe that my candor is freeing other people as well. Several really strong, accomplished, and beautiful women have contacted me to say that they too have been abused and that they have left relationships recently because of me telling my story. What happened to me is called separation violence: a person becomes violent because they cannot deal with being left. In my case, I don't think he wanted another man to ever be attracted to me, so he destroyed my face and my body. He succeeded temporarily because I cannot imagine any man wanting me at this point.

At any rate, I have to be honest and say that although he didn't knock me around daily, in retrospect, he did try to knock my self-esteem down in ways. He would say little things to diminish my accomplishments, skills, or intelligence, but he would then mask it by praising me and showering with love, gifts etc. When I would question him, he would say, "babe, you know I was just kidding...come on stop being sensitive"; and so I would let it pass. Most human dysfunction can be directly related to insecurity and low self-esteem. His insecurities manifested all the time, but I guess I overlooked them because I was probably still dealing with some of my own. I need more time to process how I got here, how I allowed this man to nearly destroy me. In retrospect, there were so many warning signs.

Thursday October 24, 2013

The human part of me often asks the question, "Why me?" Out of all the evil, hateful, vain, backstabbing, criminal-minded, miserable people in the world, why would *I* have to be damaged to this degree? Why would I have to suffer at this level? I have done absolutely nothing to deserve this, so why me? , but then my spiritual self responds to my question with "Why not you, Christy?" And then immediately my mind flashes back to the sound of a young child's piercing screams that I remember hearing while I was in the burn unit at Grady. My mother later told me that it was a 3 year old girl who had suffered 3rd degree burns to over 80 percent of her body from being trapped in a house fire, and she died after two weeks. That 3-year old never got a chance to commit even a single act of sin, and yet she suffered and she died. I had 43 years of beauty, I have experienced love, I have traveled and seen beautiful things, I got to be a mother, I had 14 years of marriage, I have been successful, I have lived well, I have earned my degrees, I have a meaningful career, I have had a great life, and most importantly, I *lived*, so although I will never look the same again, there is still more of life to enjoy. That 3-year old will never get a chance to experience any of that, so why not me? This does not change the fact that I am human and still pissed off, but it does put things into perspective, and it keeps me from going straight cuckoo. Thank you, Holy Spirit.

Friday October 25, 2013

Two of my favorite movies are *The Shawshank Redemption* and *The Count of Monte Cristo*. In both movies the characters were set up by their enemies and sentenced to prison for crimes they did not commit. Well I'm feeling a lot like them right now. I feel like I've been set up, hoodwinked, bamboozled and sentenced to a metaphorical prison sentence, but just like them both, my mind is brilliant, imaginative, and strong. Even within this "cell" I know how to take mini meditative trips with my mind. I have been to Egypt, Tuscany, Brazil, and Hawaii. In fact, I just got back from Hawaii a few minutes ago. It was lovely and breezy, with white sand and blue skies. I think that I may go visit there again tonight. Like Andy Dufresne in *The Shawshank Redemption* and the prince in *The Count of Monte Cristo*, my goal is freedom and every day I am planning and plotting my escape back to my life because my life is worth fighting for. Just as Andy did, I will carry out the bricks of this prison wall one by one, and when I have broken through this wall, I will emerge from the sewer like new. You will not even know that I have been through hell. Like Andy, I will be basking in the sunshine on that beautiful far away beach, and I will see my friends again because as Martin Luther King Jr. said, "Unearned suffering is redemptive." I will be redeemed – I will be set free.

Saturday October 26, 2013

I know some really good men. I think that's why I will not let that one bad one make me bitter. I have too many examples of good men around me.

Good does not mean perfect. I have been divorced for years and yet my ex-husband has been here for me since the day this happened. He held my hand in ICU for two months straight, went home and took care of our kids, and juggled his job. People often ask, how the heck did you end up divorced and with that acid-throwing nut? Well, because people make mistakes sometimes, and good people are not always good together, and my ex-husband and I are better as friends and co-parents. I asked him why he has been there for me after all that we've been through. His reply was, "Because you took care of me, our kids, and our home for all those years…because I know if I ever got sick or really needed help, you would be there for me…because when you are broken and not whole, our children are broken and not whole, so it is my mission to help you get whole again, as my wife or not….also because being here for you is just the right thing to do." The father of my children is a really good man.

Sunday October 27, 2013

I can remember as young as 4 years old being able to feel the presence of God. I can remember praying and seeking His approval long before I ever understood religion or could read the Bible. I just knew that God was there. My son is the same way. As I grew older my ego, my intellect and the world would often sever that intimate relationship that I naturally felt with God, and just like most people, I have sinned and backslid my entire life. I have straddled the spiritual fence and sometimes even analyzed my walk with Christ. It is easy and fun to be a sinner, it really is. In fact, Satan leaves me alone when I'm acting like a straight fool. But evil comes after me with a vengeance when I am trying to live right and when I am diligently seeking God. I have been running away from holiness my entire life, afraid of the responsibility that comes with it. Because of my innate goodness and potential for holiness, evil has been on my heels chasing me my entire life. I've been caught in the middle, stuck between sinner and saint. Wherever there is a crack – the loss of my child, the loss of my marriage, my money, my career, my beauty – evil will attack. It hits us where our treasures are. There are times like these when you have to make a choice. I can't straddle the fence now because there is too much at stake. I am in too much trouble this time and my earthly daddy can't fix this. I need a supernatural miracle; I need my Father in heaven. I am choosing God, and I choose Jesus because calling on His name works for me. Things change and I get peace when I call upon His name. Christ truly is in Christy now.

Monday October 28, 2013

Today is the six-month mark – six more months until the new me. My doctor won't start reconstructing my face until I've healed for a year so April 2014 is the magic month, the month that the new Christy begins. I wonder what the new me will be. I thought of changing my name to symbolize the drastic change in my appearance after surgeries, and also because I'm a middle aged woman with a little girl's name, ha. But Christ is the root word of my name, so I'm staying with Christy.

I haven't reached acceptance of this whole calamity, but every day I get a little closer and I cry a little less. I have no clue what stage of grief I'm in at the moment. I believe that it is the bargaining stage, but I'm not sure because I'm the one in it, instead of being the counselor watching it. I am trying really hard to let go of the old me, but I don't want to do it because I liked her. She was cute, but I have to let her go if I ever want to truly embrace this new self.

I had a bit of normalcy this weekend. Elon is getting better with this whole Freddy Krueger look that I've got going on, so I was able to spend the entire weekend with the kids for first time in 6 months. I slept in my own bed for the first time, I cooked for them, I got them ready for school; it was nice feeling like a mom again. I have to go now; baby girl wants to play UNO with me, our favorite thing.

Wednesday October 30, 2013

I have read a lot of books; my preference in reading is spirituality, psychology, or self-improvement. I have very little interest in reading fiction. Heck, my life is stranger than fiction, so who needs to read a book for that? The only fiction I have read in the past few years was "50 Shades of Grey" and that was because it is a bit psychological and because as a counselor I was interested in how women's libidos were being enhanced just by reading the book. Increased sex drive is self-improvement right? I say all this to say that I don't read just for intelligence, I read for growth. I believe that my primary goal for this life time is self-awareness and spiritual growth, and although this current situation derived from evil, I am ultimately "the master of my fate and the captain of my soul." All of this is a part of my overall growth. I have decided to take this evil thing and flip it, reframe it, defeat it, stare it down, use it for my growth, and try to remain gracious in the process. I am mind, body, and soul, so I am bigger than what happened to me. It happened to my body; it did not happen to all of me because my mind is stronger than my body, and unlike my body, my soul can never be burned or disfigured. My soul is indestructible; it is infinite. Odds are that I will be human, ticked off, and not feeling the spiritual stuff tomorrow, but such is life.

It is easier to love yourself when things are well and you are at your best, but if you can love yourself when you have lost everything; your job, your money, your mate, your looks, the respect of others...I mean everything, then my dears, you have what is called self-esteem. True self-esteem is loving one's self no matter what you have, and even if no one else does. When I was a counselor I told my clients that if they could love themselves right there in that valley, then they would be head over heels and crazy in love with themselves when they reached the top.

I realize that I lowered my standards drastically with Drew, not because I had to, but because I thought that he might be worth it. As it turned out, he was not worth it at all. I will never again lower my standards. Our standards don't have to be ridiculously high, but it is important that they be based on what we need, want, and deserve in our lives. It is important to know what our standards are, not our mama's, our sister's, our brother's, our cousin's, or our friend's standards. What are *your* standards? What is it that you *must* have in your life and in your relationships to be okay? I have learned my lesson in this area.

I am literally growing at the speed of light. I was thinking about how glad I am that I was discovering who I truly am before this happened to me. Right now I don't have what I look like, what I do for a living, or who I'm in a relationship with; I don't even have my daily role as a mother because I am isolated from my children. All I have right now is who I am, so that is what I have to work with. I am gracious, I am kind, I am love, I am brave, I am insightful, I am conscious, I am peace, I am light, I am a poet, I am a writer, and I am a fighter. I am what I am...

Thursday October 31, 2013

We buried Kayla on this day in 2001. I have never liked Halloween, and dislike it even more now. I have decided not to be sad about her today, but to be grateful for the two amazing children that God allowed me to keep. I am so glad that I put in the time and energy with Chris and Elon up until this point. I have been preparing them to be brave little Christian soldiers without even realizing the battle they would have to fight. I would not say this if it were not true, but I have fantastic kids. I actually enjoy conversations with my kids, they are not a burden to me at all. They are both interesting, intelligent, and hilariously funny. I am so glad that I will get a chance to see them grow into adults. I will see them go to college, I will see them get married, and I will see them raise their own children. That is worth living for, and that is why the alternative is not an option. I want to live to see them live…

Friday November 1, 2013

I am uncomfortable every second of every minute of every day. I am burned over twenty percent of my body; it does not look good and it does not feel good. This goes way beyond having a pretty face; I just want to look normal and feel good again. What gets me through the day is the belief that this is only temporary. I can get through anything in life, even an ugly and uncomfortable existence, as long as I can visualize an end to it. I can see myself on the other side of this. I am allowing myself to suffer publically so that when I do get through this seemingly impossible thing, everyone will know that God is who He says He is…

Saturday November 2, 2013

I love being a woman, I really do. I miss my high-heeled shoes, my gold rush lip gloss, my Mary Kay mineral powder, my eye shadows, my lovely jewelry, my fly clothes that fit my curves just right. I miss the way men would take a double look when I walked by, and some women too…ha. It all sounds shallow and a little vain. But I don't care – I miss being pretty. Prior to him destroying my face I had a hard time taking compliments and calling myself pretty because I value humility and I deplore vanity. But I can now with pride say that I was truly pretty, because I am no more, at least not on the outside. My inside, my core is prettier than before.

Sunday November 3, 2013

I am gracious because I am surrounded by grace. I love well because I have been loved so well. I falter in some areas, but loving people is what I do better than anything. I take it seriously because I believe that love conquers all and transcends time. Corny maybe, but I believe it. Mary Kay Ashe said that every person we meet has an invisible sign on their head that says "make me feel special." Making those around me feel special and loved has been my goal.

The absence of love creates insecurity within us. You can typically trace any dysfunction in adulthood back to a lack of love in childhood. Everyone that I have ever encountered in my business or personal life has received love in the form of my service to them. When I am with a client, no one in the world matters to me more than they do in that moment. When I am with my kids, they know that they are cherished, even when I have to correct or punish them; I never let the day end without them knowing that my disappointment is temporary but my love is eternal. When I am in a relationship, I give it my all until there is nothing left to give. My dog is even spoiled rotten and thinks that he is the king of all poodles. Going forward, I will not change the way that I love and treat people, but I will change who I decide to give that love to. T.D. Jakes said that it never works when a ten-gallon lover is trying to love someone with only one pint to give, because the ten-gallon lover will never get full. Overall, my selections in relationships have been good. This last one was me trying to care for a person that had never learned to love himself, which never works. I have learned that lesson in the worst way. Hurt people do indeed hurt people.

Monday November 4, 2013

The media mentioned that when the attack happened to me, I was pursuing my dream career as a substance abuse counselor...not. Ask any substance abuse counselor and they will tell you that there is nothing dreamy about helping people get off drugs. I am a Master's-level Nationally Certified

Mental Health Counselor. Substance abuse counseling does not require even a Bachelor's degree, yet it is the toughest and least paid form of counseling; it is like battling demons every day. My dream was to go into private practice and to work in a plush office doing relationship therapy and such. But God, with his sense of humor laughed at me and said "No, prissy little woman; you are originally from "The Bluff" and there is a reason for that. You will go work with all male ex-offenders, drug addicts, the men living up under the bridge, men with HIV, men who the world has given up on and who have given up on themselves." I said, "Seriously, Lord? I'm not qualified...I have never even tried drugs, I'm not a man, I don't have HIV, I've never been in jail or homeless...and I'm a new a counselor." God said to me, "You know pain and that is what addiction is really about...just love them the way that I love you, unconditionally, and soon they will love themselves." Well, I was obedient, and helping these men was the most fulfilling thing that I have ever done.

Every day at STAND, I was able to manifest the glory of God that was within me. I told my clients every day that I loved them and that they were kings (and some queens). I told them that they were too precious to be poisoning their bodies with drugs and alcohol. Some of them started to believe it, and they began to heal. I met some of the most incredible souls in those rooms. I met men who were great writers and poets. I met men who were brilliant in business, men who had families and full lives prior to addiction. They were just being chased by evil and I was trying to help, and maybe that's why I needed to be stopped in my tracks. Love was working as God said that it would. I did not choose substance abuse counseling – it chose me.

Friday November 8, 2013

It is two weeks before Thanksgiving. I am still living at my mom's house recovering and giving Elon time to adjust, but I am going home to decorate my house for Christmas this weekend because Christmas makes us happy and my house needs some happiness. I am having another surgery the first week of December so I want to decorate while I am still well enough to do it. We didn't grow up with a lot of money, and we struggled a lot, but at Christmas time, my mom made sure that we had everything. Our house was like Toys R Us on Christmas morning. She gave us what we needed year round, but on Christmas, my brother and I got what we truly wanted. I remember the year that I got my Easy Bake Oven, my Dancerella doll, my Barbie townhouse, and my shiny red 10-speed bike. Mom saved up for months and sometimes worked a second job to make sure that we had a good Christmas. This is why I love Christmas so much, it's not because of the gifts but because it reminds me of feeling plenty instead of lack. It is also the time when my family gets together and everyone is happy. I have tried to create this feeling for my kids since they were born. In general, I go to great lengths to create happy memories for them, and I don't want 2013 to be remembered just as the year that their mom got burned; nope, not on my watch. It is not about the gifts. It's about the feelings that the holiday season evokes. This year will be different because I am different and I am not well, but 6 months ago, I didn't think that I would even make it to December. Against all odds, I did make it. I am doing as much as I can to make this year as normal as possible for Chris and Elon, and I am starting this weekend so that they can have an entire month of lights and splendor, even though I won't be there daily. I'm doing it because I lived, because I feel like it, and because I can. I will have their Gran Gran, Connie to help me. She is also a Christmas queen and loves the holidays as much as I do, so it will be fun. I'm excited to be going home and doing something that feels normal.

Sunday November 10, 2013

Today I have been researching acid burn survivors and watching clips and documentaries of their recovery process. It's kind of twisted but I am obsessed with trying to find someone who has been burned as badly as I have been, and had a successful outcome. Most of the women I have seen have been strikingly beautiful. In most cases, the acid was thrown directly in their faces to make them unattractive and undesirable as in my case. Countless women from all over the world have been attacked by acid. Seeing these women who were once so beautiful makes me sad, mad, and more eager to fight back. I am worse than most of the women that I have seen, which is somewhat disheartening. The best case has been the story of Katie Piper in the UK. She is my new inspiration because she seems to have a spirit similar to my own. It is the inside that ultimately saves the outside of

65

us all. I have these few positive things going for me: 1. I am a fighter and I will not stop until everything possible has been done legally, medically, and financially to rebuild my life. 2. I am in the U.S. and not Pakistan, India, or another country where women are treated like dogs. Our legal system is flawed, but at least we have one and women have rights in the United States. 3. I have a support system of family, friends, and even total strangers. 4. I have a very strong mind, and I will not let fear nor emotion defeat me. 5. Unlike many victims, I have a voice and I am not afraid to face my abuser. 6. I have motivators that keep me wanting to wake up daily, like my two children. 7. I have faith and I am expecting a miracle, but I love myself unconditionally and eventually I will be strong enough to accept whatever face and body I have, and whatever God's will is for me and my life. This is what I am working with.

Monday November 11, 2013

What is the first thing you do when a person's name is mentioned? Your brain automatically tries to picture the person's face right? That's because a name and a face are the primary identifiers, unless you are blind. My body is burned, but I can cover that with clothing. I cannot cover my face, I need my face to function in society! He did not just take my beauty, he took my face. He robbed me of a large part of my identity. I am unrecognizable, and it is unreal. Imagine never again having the face that God gave you, the face that your children have seen their whole lives. Looking at former pictures of myself is like looking at an old friend, a friend that I never got a chance to say goodbye to. What amount of jail time can make up for this? What kind of spirit could even conjure up such a thing as this? It is still inconceivable to me. I could not do this to my worst enemy, and I was a good friend to this man, too good of a friend. Andrew Lee Fordham Jr. threw acid in my face and he did not slip and fall, that is the truth. Beware of extremely jealous and insecure people, for they may hurt you...

Wednesday November 13, 2013

Yesterday, my heart was so heavy that I had no words. I had to go deep within, to that place within my soul where God dwells, and just rest there in the Palm of His Hands; in silence and stillness. After a while, I emerged with a peace that I cannot explain, a peace that surpasses all understanding. I also emerged with a renewed attitude of gratitude. I am grateful because in spite of it all, I would never have known just how loved I am if this had not happened. I am grateful that Elon's love for me is allowing her to conquer her fears so that I can be with her more. I am grateful that Chris is so strong and wise for his young age, he is truly my comforter at times. I am grateful that I have such an amazing brother in Quinn, whom I love so much. I am grateful that Machon is such a nurturing father, and I never have to worry about our children when they are with him. I am grateful that my mom is still alive and well because she has been my saving grace. I am grateful for just waking up every day because as long as I keep waking up there is possibility. I am grateful that I had such an awareness of self before this happened. I am grateful for the kindness of others; people are truly showing me the God in them. Lord, I am especially grateful for that future day when the pain is no more, when my scars have become badges of courage, when my beaming smile returns, when my joy is renewed, when my kids have bliss again, when my test becomes my testimony, and when my story is used for Your glory. Once again I am thanking You in advance because I know that day is coming for me. I trust You Lord, with all that I am.

Saturday November 16, 2013

"I Finally Made It Back Home"

I started coming home on the weekends a few weeks ago and spending time with the kids. It has felt strange and awkward having my ex-husband live in my home and raise our kids, while I only come home to visit them on the weekends. This has been so unnatural, but is it what Elon needed to get used to being in my presence full-time. My face is still disturbing for her, but I can see her love fighting through her fear. I can see how hard she's been trying to cope with this. No child should have to go through this. She called me the other day and said, "Mommy, I'm strong enough now, I'm tired of you being away, please come home now." So I went home.

"Home"
Home for me is the scent of ginger peach
hitting me as I walk through the door
the glimmer of my cherry hardwood floor
It is clean and pristine with tasteful decor
...and windows galore
It is Friday night movies with the kids
It is Saturday morning clean up with Mr. Clean
It is Sundays with cornbread and collard greens
It is the sound of Miles or Coltrane blasting away
It is a steaming hot bubble bath after a long day
It is slipping into crisp and cool white sheets
It is my dog Sam falling fast asleep at my feet.
It is a center piece of sunflowers or yellow tulips
It is being alone, but not feeling lonely.
It is an infusion of warmth with
the colors orange, olive, and gold
It is relaxing on the couch and
just letting the day unfold
Home for me is Chris and Elon
Home is simply that...it is home

Whenever my kids are feeling sad or sorry for me, I look them straight in their eyes and say, "Your mom is a badass little "B,," and if anyone can get through this it would be me," and then we all crack up laughing and the moment passes. It is our running joke, and I have given them permission when they feel uncomfortable in dealing with their peers and the public when questioned too much. They both can say "Thanks for your concern but my mom is a badass little "B" and if anyone can get through this, she can," then say no more. I want them to emerge from this tragedy feeling empowered, and I can only do this by showing them what empowerment looks like. We are not victims, we are survivors. We are powerful beyond measure.

Sunday November 17, 2013

Children can be annoying, expensive, loud, messy, inconvenient, time consuming – in fact, they can be all consuming, and one day when they leave you may just get your heart broken. So, I totally respect people who have decided to never have children because children are a huge responsibility, but I recommend them to anyone unselfish enough to love them and care for them. I would cry all day every day if I did not have my children to keep me focused on them and not on me. At this moment I feel like lying in bed and crying, but I can't because Elon needs me to help her with her 4H project. I will cry when they leave for school tomorrow. On those days when I can't imagine living like this, when I consider the possibility of dying, I snap out of it when I imagine my kids without a mother, and when I imagine missing all of the important events in their lives. They love me in spite of my funny looking face; they love me unconditionally. Please have kids if still you want them. You are not too old, and even if you are single it is okay. There may be a child somewhere waiting for you to come and get them. Sometimes we have to create a "new normal" when things don't work out as we planned. And yes mine are starting to tap dance on my one last nerve again, but it is okay because it means that we are approaching normal.

Monday November 18, 2013

I love a thick chick with confidence. This girl Amber Riley on Dancing with the Stars is the Truth Ruth. She is an older version of my baby girl, Elon. My plus-sized little girl has more confidence and self-esteem than some super models. As a parent, self-esteem has always been key for me, and I have been working on this with my kids since day one.

I knew that the world would try to tear them down the moment that they left the house, and it did in the form of "the mean girls" in second grade. I told my Elon every day that she was beautiful and loved, but all it took was a pack of "mean girls" to make her question herself. The bullying lasted about two weeks before we both said "enough," and we came up with responses to every mean thing that could be said to her. "You're fat!" Elon says, "Meat is for men, bones are for dogs, I like my thickness." Or she says, "God made me this way, so if you have a problem with me then you have a problem with God. Bam!" We came up with tons of comebacks because all she needed was to feel that she was armored against the hate. Hate caught her off guard and broke her heart because I had been teaching her kindness, so hate was foreign to her. After shutting the bullies down a few times, they stopped messing with my baby. Now she just gives them "the look," and they know to walk away quietly. Mission self-esteem accomplished.

Tuesday November 19, 2013

Earlier I was watching The Katie Couric Show from November 13th about face transplants. I'm burned badly enough to probably get a face transplant, but I would be too far down on the list and it would likely take years because although my entire face is burned, most of my features are still in place; my eyes, nose, and mouth are all where they should be. Generally, people who receive face transplants have to be on immune suppressants for the rest of their lives, which means that they are always open to disease and sickness. If I have a choice, I would rather be less attractive than sick all the time. The burn survivors featured on the show were missing their faces entirely. There are some truly hateful, evil, and sick people in this world. But there are also people like the ones on this show that simply blow me away with their courage and emotional fortitude. My situation is pretty jacked up, and I have a long recovery ahead of me, but I have made some progress. There are some people much worse than I am. My hope is that I have as much courage as they do. All of the skin for my face is coming from my stomach, imagine that. The negatives are that I will never look the same again, and I won't look good in sleeveless or low cut tops anymore, so no more sexy for me. The positives are that I will never wrinkle on my face; at 80 I may look 40. I will have an even tighter stomach; I get a tummy tuck by default because all of the grafts are coming from there. This is all so unusual, but it is real, and it is my life right now. It is what it is, until it ain't what it ain't.

Thursday November 21, 2013

Dr. Spence's assistant, Lori, and I spoke today. She calls me every week to check on me. She is such a beautiful spirit and so gifted at counseling burn survivors. She called today to confirm my surgery for next month. On September 11th, Dr. Spence repaired my eyes, rearranged the skin tissue on my right arm so that I could extend it, and inserted tissue expanders on each side of my abdomen. Lori was so amazed that Machon drives from McDonough to Stone Mountain every week just to inject the tissue expanders with saline. Mom is so squeamish that she nearly passes out at site of needles and blood, so Machon agreed to do it every week. He inserts a needle into the port located on each side of my waist and forces saline in the tissue expander. Each week my abdomen expands more and more. We have been doing this since I returned from my surgery in September and I now look about 6 months pregnant. As horrid as it sounds to look pregnant when I am not, I get more and more excited as my stomach expands because it means more skin tissue available to repair my face and neck. My next surgery is scheduled for next month on December 5th. This will hopefully allow me two weeks to recover in Baltimore and be well enough to fly back home before Christmas. With this next surgery, Dr. Spence will completely remove the skin from my entire neck because it is severely contracted and I have almost no movement. Just as with my eyes, this surgery is necessary for the functionality of my neck. Right now the skin from my neck is fused to my face and I can barely move my head. It is causing me discomfort and it will ultimately lead to me having long-term neck and back problems if he does not fix it now. So, the plan is that mom and I fly to Baltimore on December 4th and Dr. Spence replaces my neck on December 5th. He will remove the skin needed for my neck and then reinsert a new tissue expander so he can harvest enough skin for my remaining surgeries.

Friday November 22, 2013

I use the phrase "It is what it is" often because I take this phrase literally. I attended the Landmark Forum back in 2008 and after being locked in a room for 3 days with 60 other people, the facilitator's final words were "It is what it is." That was it; that was the point of the entire forum. Basically, life happens whether we are participants in it or not. It will keep going and things will keep happening bad and good. Life is so much harder when we push against it. I have said it before – our reaction to what happens to us is the game changer. Our response to the challenges in our lives is what determines if we are punks or powerhouses. I also believe that whatever we resist will persist, whatever you push against will keep pushing back, and whatever you focus your thoughts intently upon will keep manifesting in your life. Right now I feel like I have less control over my life, but as I have said before, there are only two things that any of us have ever had any control over and that is our behavior and how we choose to feel about ourselves, and not one more thing. It becomes exhausting trying to control the uncontrollable, so I have decided to just stop, stop resisting, be still, let go and let God...just for today. Tomorrow may be another story. I am a powerhouse, I am not a punk.

Monday November 25, 2013

The five stages of grief are: denial, anger, bargaining, depression, and acceptance. Most think of grief as only being associated with the loss of a loved one, but these stages can apply to any significant loss. The loss of a job can trigger grief, a major move or relocation, the loss of a relationship or friendship, a major illness, and any major change in life. The loss of my appearance, my career, and the normality of my daily life has felt very much like a death to me, and thus I have been going through the stages. Being a professional counselor while going through this is both a curse and a blessing. I have studied the stages and I have had several significant losses, so I understand them and I can identify them. But I also find myself overanalyzing my own emotions, which is just ridiculous. When I did the first interview with V-103, and then the one with Tom Joyner, everyone said that I sounded so strong and powerful. As I said before, my brother was upset with me because I downplayed my disfigurement and said that I was not actually in a coma. It was too soon for me to be doing interviews because my mind had not fully processed how bad my injuries were. It had only been two weeks since I saw my face for first time, and just 3 weeks after awakening from the coma. I was in complete denial. I believe that I will keep reverting back to the anger stage for a very long time to come because of the way this has affected those that I love. I believe that I am currently in the bargaining stage and steadily approaching the depression stage. The upcoming holidays are triggering bittersweet emotions because I'm glad that I made it this far, but I'm sad that I can't fully enjoy this season. The acceptance stage is my goal; this is the stage where joy resides and peace abides. When I get to this stage, I will dance like David no matter how I look.

Tuesday November 26, 2013

The Holy Spirit speaks to me in various ways. Last night Elon dreamt that I was completely renewed. She said that in her dream I looked a little different, my complexion was a shade darker, but I was pretty again. She said, "Your skin was smooth like a Barbie doll mommy." She was so excited to wake up and tell me and I believe that it gave her the peace that she needed. It is hard to explain to a 10 year who sees her mother's face completely burned, that the doctors are going to remove mommy's face and put on new skin. She has been confused as to how this will all end. The dream helped her to visualize it, and helped me to visualize it because I am just as confused. Children have a way of making things simple and real. Several other people have had similar dreams, including me. As I said before, I can't see myself with scars in any of my dreams.

Another strange thing happened yesterday. I was sleeping and was suddenly awaked by a minister on TV. His exact words were "YOU WILL BE COMPLETELY RESTORED AND MADE NEW, AND LIKE JOB, YOU WILL RECIEVE DOUBLE FOR YOUR TROUBLE, IN JESUS' NAME!" It was like he was screaming directly at me. It was so loud that it woke me up out of a deep sleep, and I don't remember watching that channel before I fell asleep. Creepy, but the Holy Spirit in effect once again. My mom, Inger, Connie, and several other people have been saying these exact words to me for months, so when I heard them from this man; it was just further confirmation. All I have to do is wait on the Lord and be of good courage...

Friday November 29, 2013

I spent Thanksgiving mostly alone yesterday because the kids were with Machon. I am totally fine with that, and I am so glad to be home. My kids are out shopping with their gran-gran Connie thanks to gift cards from Inger's co-workers at IHeath. I really don't care much for shopping and I really don't like crowds, but I would love to be out in the hustle and bustle today if I could, just to feel the energy of the season. Maybe next year, but for now I will just appreciate being able to peer out of my bedroom window and watch the pretty yellow, orange, and brown leaves fall from my trees. I slept through spring and part of summer, but I am wide awake to see this lovely fall and I am awaiting the chill of winter. When spring rolls around again the new Christy will begin; I will become a new flower...a yellow tulip, perhaps.

Saturday November 30, 2013

In December 2012, I journaled that I was so happy and excited about 2013 that I was about to burst. I had completed graduate school, I had passed the national counselor exam, and I was loving my job. I was truly happy this time last year. I think the devil must have been listening because he completely jacked up 2013, I mean he just shattered it. I believe that I will just keep my thoughts about 2014 to myself and pray for a better future. The evil one is always waiting and lurking, just waiting for a chance to kill, still, and destroy; it is his job. I was doing meaningful work as a counselor. I was truly helping people change their lives. I feel as if Satan went to God about me the same way that he went to him about Job. He probably said " If I burn her body, steal her beauty, take her money and her job, isolate her from everyone including her children, I bet she would turn on you Lord." I guess God could have said, "You can jack up her life, but you cannot kill her." I honestly do not know what the powers that be think of me. I am just speculating and rationalizing. This is what people do in the bargaining stage of grief: we try to make sense of the senseless.

Sunday December 1, 2013

I sleep like a baby every night, but mornings are difficult for me. Reality hits me like a brick every morning. Today was a little worst because I have to say goodbye to the kids again today and head off for another surgery this week. Every goodbye reminds me of the morning of April 26th, which was the last time that I saw them as a whole, happy, healthy and unscarred woman. I dropped them off for school that morning not knowing that would be the last time that I would be able to drop them off, that I was about to face death, that I would not see them for months, and that would be the last time they would see "my face," so leaving them now just means more. As I write this, the Spirit just came over me and said, "But you did not die, you have a second chance to get it right." I am a little nervous about surgery, but it is necessary so I guess that I had better put my big girl panties on and keep it moving, and since I am not ready to die, I guess I had better get about the business of living. Right now, I'm just surviving and existing. This is not truly living. I know what abundant life looks like because I have had it. It is what God promised me, it is what I deserve, and it is what I will have again...in the name of Jesus.

Tuesday December 3, 2013

I'm leaving for Baltimore again tomorrow for two weeks and I have not packed one thing. I don't know how I have survived in this life being this way, but I don't think that I'll be changing anytime soon. If the kids were going with me, I would have packed them a week ago. I don't know why I slack on me, but I am totally on point with other people. What I am doing right now is avoiding what I need to do, which is pack my dang bag, by doing something easy like posting on Facebook. I am flawed, but at least I know it.

Monday December 9, 2013

I am in Baltimore recovering from surgery. These surgeries are almost more than I can bear. I try really hard to remain positive and not go to dark places, even during my suffering, but I am truly suffering today and all I can think about is the physical, emotional, and mental discomfort that I have to endure every day, when all I did was back away from a relationship that was no longer good for me. When I get through this current healing process I am fighting even harder to get this man charged because no one deserves to be hurt this much. People go to jail for J-walking, yet this man is still free after disfiguring me and destroying my life. This type of assault happens to thousands of women across the globe, but rarely in the US and almost never in Georgia, so it is harder to prosecute. I will set the precedent, I will be the first, and I will fight even if it means showing the world just how burned and disfigured I really am. No one who sees this could possibly believe that this man was not trying to hurt me, because it is just that bad. I am weak and extremely uncomfortable but I will not stop until I get justice. I have no bitterness, but he needs to be punished for this. This was inhumane.

Thursday December 12, 2013

Dr. Spence replaced my entire neck with skin grafted from the left side of my abdomen. I am looking like the bride of Frankenstein right now. I have been stitched up, stapled up, pinned up, glued up and jacked up. I am literally being rebuilt, piece by piece. I thank God for the possibility though, and for this not happening 60 years ago because although I will never again have my same face (unless God waves His hand over me and makes it happen), thanks to God and modern medicine, I will hopefully have a face that I can live with. As for now, the only thing cute on me is my pink twinkly toes. Thank God for my cute feet!

Friday December 13, 2013

Nelson Mandela transitioned this week. I figure if he could survive 27 years of bondage, emerge unbroken, and go from prisoner to president within one lifetime, then anything is possible. If I could have just one cup of his courage, an ounce of his anointing, a teaspoon of his faith, and a centimeter of his grace, then I can survive anything. He was 95, so I am not sad that he died, I am just so glad that he lived.

I can live more boldly and fearlessly now because I have faced both the devil and death and won. When I meet them both again, I will not be so caught off guard.

Today I am praying for the parents that lost their babies a year ago in the Sandy Hook shooting. I have had to bury one of my own seed, and yet I can only imagine their pain.

It is a winter wonderland in Baltimore. It is snowing again here for the 3rd time this week, but people are out and about like the sun is shining. If it were snowing like this in Atlanta, the entire city would be shut down. I like the DC area, but I am a Georgia girl through and through. I love that we have such great weather in Atlanta, I love that we experience all four seasons fully, but some years we barely have to wear heavy coats. Atlanta would be perfect if we had the ocean, but at least we don't have to worry about typhoons, earthquakes, tornadoes and such. I love that there are so many successful brown people in Atlanta. I love that I could own a mini-mansion for less than 250K, and that I could flip houses like pancakes until the market went south. I love the mixture of city and country in Atlanta. I love going out seeing masses of beautiful brown people, dressed to the nines and trying to outdo each other. It all sounds so shallow, but I like to see us looking good because there are so many negative images of brown people in the media. I love having a birthplace that is so rich and deeply rooted in social change. I love that I grew up with Maynard Jackson's kids, Julian Bond's kids, and Marvin Arrington's kids because these men showed me possibility as a kid. I love turning on the news and seeing beautiful brown Lisa Rayam. If you can't make it as a brown person in Atlanta, then you will likely have a hard time anywhere. I love all people so I love that Atlanta is so diverse. I am ready to go home.

Sunday December 15, 2013

I am still recovering at the Holiday Inn in Baltimore, and I'm feeling a little better each day. I should be home just before Christmas. I am so glad I decorated the house before I left for surgery.

Mom and I just watched Mandela's glorious homecoming celebration. I am

77

happy that Mandela died as a free former president instead of a prisoner because they would have buried this amazing man in a shallow grave instead of giving him the royal home going celebration that he deserves. A man that was imprisoned with Mandela for 18 years said that it was the guard's mission to crush them and break their spirits every day, but instead of Mandela being fueled by a desire to crush them back, he was fueled by the desire to never be crushed. This inspired me and spoke volumes because it explains how I feel about what happened to me. He tried to crush me because my light was too bright for his darkness. I have anger because it is natural, but I am not fueled by hate, bitterness, or revenge. I am fueled by an overwhelming desire to not be broken. This has bent me, but it will not break me. God will step in before that happens. My greatest assets are my mind and my faith.

Rest in peace Nelson Mandela, well done.

Monday December 16, 2013

I have been with my mother here in Baltimore for almost two weeks. She never leaves my side. I have not spent this much time with her since I was two years old. Strangely we don't get on each other's nerves (much) because we don't just love each other, we actually like each other. This is one positive out of this negative; my mom and I have gotten reacquainted as girlfriends. I tell her every chance that I get how much I love and appreciate her. Her reply is always, "I appreciate you too; you will always be my baby and never a burden to me." I believe her and she is the only person that I trust to take care of me. I will be honored to take care of her when the time comes. She is praying for me even when I'm not praying for myself. She prayed me back to life. Her faith is so strong and she believes so strongly that I will be completely healed that I have no choice but to believe it. We were not this close before, but if either one of us passed away tomorrow, nothing would be left unsaid.

I'm looking out of my window here into the shopping district across the street. The shoppers are out in a frenzy, gathering their Christmas gifts and all I can think is...at least I have an excuse not to be out in that mess this year. I love Christmas, but it can be so stressful, especially if you are a last minute shopper who has a need to buy the whole earth a gift like me. My kids will have what they want, but all I have to give my large and extended family this year is my love. I hope it's enough!

Tuesday December 17, 2013

Writing is my way of fighting...

Two more wake ups and then I am headed back to Atlanta and my precious munchkins. I made it through my 8th surgery, with many more to come. My stitches come out tomorrow. Doctor Spence says that he may be able to start on my face before the one year mark in March, hopefully. It will be dependent upon how this current skin graft heals. The year 2014 will be an entire year of rebuilding and constant surgeries. It will take the entire year to reconstruct my face (deep sigh). I can't even imagine what I will look like in the end, but it has to be better than this.

Wednesday December 18, 2013

My stitches are out, and thanks to my stomach, I have a new neck. It all sounds oh so cray-cray. Next, I get new cheeks. I may start revealing pictures of myself after the next surgery, maybe not. I made a decision just now. Drew's mission was to steal my beauty and my way of life, in an effort to steal my joy because he had no joy. Well, my looks are gone and my way of life is totally different, but I have decided to steal bits and pieces of my life and my joy back. When I get home I'm going to my park where I used to run 3 miles a day, and although I can't run right now, I'm going to walk around the lake and I'm going to feed the geese like I used to. They won't care how I look as long I've got bread crumbs. Yes, that would bring me joy. It doesn't take much for me. I simply cannot wait until life is good and I'm whole again to start stealing my joy back. I must do it now. You must do it now....

Thursday December 19, 2013

I have made it back to the "A," but I am feeling some type of way today; not a good, bad, or sad way...just a way. I feel like I just made it through another hell and I'm just sitting here like, now what? I am in what Iyanla Vanzant calls "the hallway." I am in that space between my disaster and my destiny, that space where real "soul work" is done, and when I am done...God can you please open the door at the end of the hallway? Pretty please...?

Friday December 20, 2013

Christmas will be very different this year. I still have not seen most of my family so it will just be me and the kids, my brother, and my mom. It will not be Toys-R-Us at my house this year either, but between Inger and my in-laws, the kids will be fine. I'm staying home all day and it will be really quiet and relaxed, very unlike the hoopla of yester-years. I have a large and loud family, but I'm not up for all that this year. I will see each of them one by one as I get more comfortable with my scars, and as I have more surgeries. I don't want to have to deal with other people's emotions on Christmas, I have enough of my own right now. They love me so they will understand. I'm establishing a "new normal" this year and who knows, I may just end up liking a quiet and private Christmas.

Sunday December 22, 2013

I'm so thankful to be back home with the kids, but I'm in a funk today and I'm trying to snap out of it. I do not like what this does to my kids. As hard as they try, looking at me still breaks their hearts. I can't go to any of their events. Chris had a game this morning and I couldn't go. It just sucks. My baby girl walked in on me crying this morning so of course she started to cry and then I had to manage her feelings in addition to my own. It's just too much sometimes. I hate sadness. I am a happy person by nature. I must snap us out of this. It's time for a game of UNO, it works every time. Children heal best through play and so do I.

Monday December 23, 2013

Yesterday was a bit rough, but today is better. I opened up Facebook just now and the first post that I saw was a post from my friend Stacy Chandler Franklin. She has been bravely battling cancer the entire time that I have been going through my battle. Well, she won! She has been in stage 3 cancer for the past 6 months. We have both been trying to heal with grace and dignity. She had a radical mastectomy last week and the doctors just called and said that she is now cancer free! Praise God! This made my day. Just as I have, Stacy has been publically praising God through her pain and struggle. I believe that we do it for the same reason, which is to let everyone know that *God did that*. I am so elated for her, and I am expecting my miracle. As I said, yesterday was a rough day, but if it were not for my bad days, I would have less appreciation for my good days. My friend surviving makes this a really good day.

Tuesday December 31, 2013

I need a T-shirt that says "I Survived 2013." This was supposed to be one of the best years of my life because I had accomplished some major life goals and I was truly happy, but instead it ended up being the most hellish and challenging year of my life. Still, in the midst of the pain, I have learned so much this year. I learned to actually live the clichés that have always driven me nuts like "take one day at a time," "what doesn't kill you, makes you stronger," "God is in control," "beauty is within," "simple things are the best things," "God never gives you more that you can handle," "time heals all wounds," and "love conquers all." Well, as it turns out they are all true, and I am a living witness. The operative word here is "living," because although my life has been forever changed, so many people did not make it to see 2014. But I did, I survived 2013, and if you are reading this then so did you. I'm so glad that we made it – we made it through.

Wednesday January 1, 2014

Dear Reader,

I never leave things unsaid anymore, so this has to be said. You are loved, you are beautiful inside and out, you are powerful beyond measure, you are perfectly imperfect and fine just the way you are. You are a marvelous work in process and worthy of greatness, you are deserving of every wonderful thing that is possible in this life. Even on your worst day, you are better than most. You have more love and goodness in your pinky finger than some people have in their whole body. You are incredible, brilliant, insightful, and when this life is over it will matter that you lived. There is no one else in this entire world quite like you. You walk around every day with a piece of God inside of you...He is not just around you...His spirit dwells

81

within you, and this is what makes you so powerful. You can manifest anything that you desire, you have that ability, so use it. It does not matter what you have done in the past, how you look, how old you are, or where you are right now, you can do anything. I just wanted you to know this, just in case no one else tells you because I wish that someone had told me, and because I love you.

Friday January 3, 2014

I had a bit of a setback last week and had to have emergency surgery this past Saturday, which may affect my upcoming facial surgery in March. I think that the turn of this new year has also triggered the fourth stage of grief, which is depression. I knew it was coming. I have always been excited at the beginning of a new year, filled with excitement, anticipation, plans, resolutions, and a chance to start fresh, but it doesn't feel that way this year. Right now I am filled with uncertainty and because I have so little control, it is nearly impossible to make long term plans. In the past I thought I had control and I was pretty good about laying out my future. I planned almost every aspect of my life, from marriage to career to even the timing of my children, but if you ever want to see God laugh, try planning your own life without His consultation. I am now forced to trust and follow Him completely. I have no New Year resolutions; all I want this year is to get a new face, to maintain my sanity in the process, and to maintain happiness and well-being for my two children. That is all, I no longer care about making the million dollar club in real estate, or winning a pink Caddy in Mary Kay, or even being counselor of the year. I just want those three things.

Saturday January 4, 2014

I told my mom that I don't know how I'm going to make it through the next year. I'm tired of being ugly, uncomfortable, and isolated and sick of hospitals and surgeries and all of it, and she said "It's been 8 months already, you've already been through months of hell and you will get through the next 12 months the same way you got through the last 8 months...day by day...and with the help of God." Like every nurse at Emory told me as I was learning to walk again "One day at a time, Christy." I think that they must be trained to say this because every single one said it, so although I think that I may just crack up if I hear it again, there is definitely truth to it because after weeks of taking it day by day, I walked right out of that hospital. Patience is not one of my virtues and I deplore processes. I want things to happen right now. I want to drive to the store right now and get cupcakes for the kids and me because we're craving them (well, *I'm* craving them), but I cannot drive my car yet, so I must wait on someone to bring them and I don't like depending on people.

Sunday January 5, 2014

When my daughter Kayla passed away 12 years ago, I told myself that if I could get through that, then I could get through anything. It took a while, but I got through that pain and I became stronger, wiser, more empathetic, and more compassionate because of it. That experience led me into counseling; it gave me the emotional fortitude necessary to help others walk through their pain. I am what we refer to in the counseling profession as a "wounded healer." There is nothing more painful than losing a child, and this situation seems similar. When you lose a child, you feel like you're losing a part of yourself, and that is what this feels like. I feel like I lost a part of myself, and not just the exterior, but the interior, the quality of life, the function and mobility of my body. That light inside of me is fading a little. This is what depression looks like. I have entered the depression stage of my grief.

I will never give up and throw in the towel because I love God, myself, my kids, and life too much, but I also love and understand myself enough truly *feel* every inch of this process, even the depression. I wish that I was well enough to go running. Running is what saved me when Kayla passed away. It releases endorphins and keeps the mood elevated. I would run every day until I felt better, and as a bonus, I also lost 30 pounds in three months. I had lost every pound of my pregnancy weight within a matter of months. In fact, I got so fit and fine that Machon could not resist me and I got knocked-up with Elon the spring after Kayla's passing.

As a part of therapy during my time as a counselor, I helped my clients put together a "survival tool kit" to help them get through the hardest days of addiction recovery. Now I need my own tool kit to help me get through the roughest days of my recovery. Life is such a trip. Maybe God gave me the tools to help others knowing that I would need to use some of them to help myself. My new tool kit consists of daily meditation and prayer, conversations with my friends LaNese, Jonell, and Inger, interacting on Facebook , playing UNO with the kids, long hot showers, minimal stretching and exercise, walking around the lake (soon), the book of Job, music, positive talks with my surgeon, being silly with the kids, comedies, anything hilariously funny, journaling, listening to Dr. Wayne W. Dyer, Dr. Charles Stanley, T.D. Jakes and others, Almond Snickers (a must have), therapy, and focusing on other people's stuff to keep my mind off my stuff – all of these things help a little. Every survivor needs a "tool kit." If you need one, get one. You must nurture your psyche as you maneuver through the storm so that when the storm passes, you will be sane enough to truly appreciate and enjoy the sunshine.

Monday January 6, 2014

I was just "checking in" with Chris about why he never cries, wondering if he cries alone and if he needs to talk. He said, "Mom, I'm fine and I don't feel like crying...I cried when I needed to." I asked how could he be fine when everything about me and our life has changed? My 14-year old son replied, "I don't cry because I know that this is only temporary. Why cry about temporary things? I already know for sure that you are going to be okay." I talk about Elon a lot because she is the one with the personality and over the top emotions, but Chris is my son/soulmate, critical thinking, spiritual, quiet, reserved, intuitive, indigo child. He requires little attention and watches over me like a hawk. As I said, he is the one that told me one month before this happened "Mom, I want you to be happy, but he is not right for you, I feel danger when he is around." I believed my son then, and I believe him now. This is only temporary, and we will be okay.

Tuesday January 7, 2014

I have definitely reached the depression stage. My cool Prince Chris may not need to cry, but I do! As soon as they leave for school I'm going to cry like a new born baby. I'm going to cry like someone stole my candy. I'm going to cry like a 2-year old throwing a temper tantrum – a snot dropping, cheek burning cry, a bang my head against the wall kicking and screaming kind of cry. I am Courageous Christy and this is only temporary, but right now is right now…and right now I need a long hard cry. I may even suck my thumb when I'm done.

Thursday January 9, 2014

When I woke up from that that 2-month coma 6 months ago, I was completely blind, and I could not walk, use my arms, or even feed myself. I could not bathe myself or even reposition myself in the bed. Today, I am living with third and fourth degree burns and I do not recognize myself, but I've gotten nearly everything else back. My vision is better now, I can walk, and I can take care of myself. I know that God did this.

This is how I have decided to fight depression: I'm looking for God everywhere, even in the mess. I'm looking for reasons to be grateful, even in the mess. The devil has attacked me in every area of my life – my health, my wealth, my family, my career. I have suffered more in the past 8 months than most people suffer in a life time, but I'm sticking with God no matter what because He can make the rain fall and He's going to reward me "double for my trouble," just wait and see. I have the substance of things hoped for, and the evidence of things not seen, I have faith.

Saturday January 11, 2014

I'm feeling strangely okay today…today would be a good day to finish setting up my blog and finish the kid's memory books. I'm giving each of them books of pictures of us as they were growing up so that they can have some memories of the old me, as we all try to let her go and move on to the next Christy. It is a strange phenomenon to loose one's entire outer appearance. It is kind of like dying, but not. Looking at my old pictures is like looking at a beautiful young woman that I once knew and loved, but I must let her go. I wish that yellow tulips were in season. I need some yellow tulips, but fresh sunflowers will do.

Today the glass looked half full instead of half empty, as it does on some days. Absolutely nothing changed from yesterday, except my attitude and my perception. Today I'm trying to focus on where I am right now and how close I am to where I'm going because I can do nothing about yesterday, and dwelling there is holding me back. All I have is today, and a lovely vision of tomorrow.

Sunday January 12, 2014

"Pretty No More"

Wondering what will become of me
Remembering a time when I was free
Embracing the moment and learning to just be
Missing my happiness, my joy, my bliss
The reverie of young love and sweet first kiss
Visions of yellow tulips, sunflowers,
sunrises and sunsets at the beach
A time when joy was within reach
Pretty this, pretty that, pretty no more
Evil came in and closed that door
Wondering what will become of me
Remembering a time when I was free
Embracing the moment, and learning to just be...

"Blessed"

It is hard to feel blessed while within a mess,
but I do, I still feel blessed.
I feel blessed to be loved unconditionally.
I feel blessed to be a daughter, a mother,
and a little sister to my big brother.
I feel blessed to have wonderful life-long friends
and I feel blessed to have new friends come in.
I feel blessed to have this new found voice...
even though it was not by choice.
I feel blessed that God so graciously spared my sight
I need my eyes so that I can take flight...
into this new and unfamiliar life.
It is hard to feel blessed while within a mess,
but I do, I still feel blessed.

Saturday January 18, 2014

I am still recovering and still in the depression stage of grief. I always know when I am depressed because I write poetry non-stop. But, I'm feeling momentary joy right now because my little girl just got back from getting her hair pressed and she is so happy and feeling so good about herself. She has had to wear braids (which are great) for the past 9 months because I was not there to care for her hair, and braids are easier for her dad to manage alone, but today baby girl's hair is straightened and silky and lovely. I remember what that feels like because my mom kept my hair done the same way that I have always taken care of Elon's, except for these months that I could not. Right now I have joy because I am vicariously living through her "pretty." She is pretty enough for the both of us, and pretty is not just a look, it is a feeling. My daughter *feels* pretty, and that makes me happy.

Monday January 20, 2014

I never thought I would hear myself saying this, but I want to go to work! I am supposed to be somewhere counseling someone, selling someone a house, renting someone a house, or selling someone some Mary Kay 3-in-1 Cleanser and lip gloss or something. I like making money! I feel like a fish out of water, and from the looks of it, I've got months and months of this.

Okay, that was my "human self" venting. My "higher self" continues to pray.

Lord, I am exactly where I am supposed to be. Let Your will be done in my life. Thank you for this stillness, for this life break because it is allowing me to focus on You and learn more about me. Lord, not only do I thank you for the stillness, I thank you for a warm and comfortable home that I can be still in, and for a loving family that allows me to be still and rest. Lord, I thank you for the enrichment of my mind, of my spirit, and of my relationships. Thank God for my "higher self" keeping me in check; I would be a total mess without it.

Thursday January 23, 2014

It is amazing how I can talk to some people and the sound of their voice just calms me. I get that from my best friends LaNese and Jonell because I know they always have my best interests at heart, and they are both voices of reason. I get it from my friend Cherry Collier, and of course from my cocoa butter friend.

I also got a message today from Inger that calmed me. I already knew it, but I needed to hear it today because I have been looking in the mirror too much today, and the mirror is not my friend. I have been allowing myself to look at the impossibilities. She confirmed something that I know and have said before. My situation looks impossible because of the extreme level that I have been burned, and honestly I have no clue how this can be fixed to where I can even work again or have a normal life, but it's not for me to *know*, it is for me to just *trust*. If it did not look impossible, then I would have no need to rely solely on God. Impossibility is God's specialty. Just think about it for a moment – we can do the possible things ourselves. Faith is enhanced and God is glorified when something this extreme happens. Evil started it, but God will finish it. As my friend Francis Monroe often says, "God is the best of knowers." I'm going to let God do what He does best because this situation is way "above my pay grade." I am not at all qualified to handle this alone, and I'm cool with that fact.

Monday January 27, 2014

I woke up feeling some type of way today as I typically do on Mondays because I miss working. It's strange I know, but I actually liked my job and I was doing meaningful work. Then the Spirit stepped in and reminded me that tomorrow is January 28th, the 9-month mark. My life was forever changed on April 28th, but I have lived 9 months longer than the doctors thought I ever would, so I think that I'll stop feeling sorry for my funny looking self and get on up. I'll keep on living because if I was going die, 9 months ago was the mostly likely time to do it. I'm still here, so I must have a purpose, and I guess that I had better start trying to figure out what it is. Life should be very interesting from this point forward. I have a feeling that God is up to something good. I'm a bit nervous though because if He is allowing me to go through all of this madness then it must be something extraordinary, and it will probably require a lot of courage...I just hope that I have enough. April 3rd is the date that the transformation of my face begins and the new Christy starts. I have been waiting for this date for months because it is the key to me having a life again. I will not look the same, but I will certainly look better than this, and that is progress. Anyway, my mood has improved a bit so I think that I will polish my toes a deep deep red, try to look cute, and put on my best perfume so I can feel pretty. I no longer have to look for a miracle...I *am* the miracle.

Tuesday January 28, 2014

It is 2:28 pm and at this very moment 9 months ago, Andrew Lee Fordham, Jr. changed my life forever. I want to send him a note to say "Look, I'm still here, you bent me, but you did not break me. You burned me outside, but I'm still beautiful on the inside. You took me from my children and traumatized them, but I am with them now and they are smiling again. You caused my family so much heartache and pain, but we are still standing and stronger than ever. You kept me from walking at my graduation, but I still received my degree because I had already earned it. You caused me to lose a job that I love, but my boss says I can come back as soon as I am able. You wanted to isolate me and make me unwanted and unloved, but I am loved more than ever and my relationships are even richer. You are free now, but you will never be truly free after harming a child of God. What I really want to say to him is that God wins, love wins, and I will win because I am still here and my heart is still as good as gold. You did not burn my core, so you did not win, but I will say none of these things to him because he does not deserve the air that I breathe nor the time it takes to send a note. So I say this to the universe: God wins...love wins...and I will win.

Friday January 31, 2014

It has been 9 months since I went to the nail salon. I think I may just mosey on up the street and frighten my nail salon friends. Trying to do my own pedicures is just unnatural. There are just some things in life that I woman must do, and taking care of her feet is one of them. Being well groomed is absolutely necessary for me no matter how funny my face looks. The nurses in the burn unit thought it was odd that I was burned so badly and looked so horrible, but had perfectly polished and manicured hands and feet. I

89

could hear them talking about it. One of them said, "I can tell what kind of woman she is by looking at her hands and feet, I bet she was pretty..." and all I could do was smile inside, and think..."I'm so glad I went to the salon the day before this happened." I'm a girlie-girl through and through. My nail salon friends have not seen me since I've been burned and they are very direct and somewhat insensitive, so let's see how this goes.

Sunday February 2, 2014

I like to think that I am perfectly imperfect. I am imperfection at its best. I am imperfect in every single way, and it is kind of liberating to no longer be even considering perfection as a possibility. The pressure is released. I have never had the need to be the prettiest, the finest, the smartest, the most successful person in any situation; there are just too many great people in the world to be competing with, so that would be exhausting. I get sincere delight in other people's triumphs, and jealousy and envy have never resided in me, which is why I get along with most people, but this acceptance of my own imperfection is kind of new, and pleasantly liberating. This is my lowest point in life thus far, I look the worst, I have the least amount of money, and I'm isolated. But I believe that I may be the most secure within myself at this point...odd, isn't it? I cannot let him steal my mojo – it is all that I've got left.

Wednesday February 5, 2014

You want to know how to get through something horrific? You tell on it, you talk about it until it no longer owns and controls you. That is why therapy works...that is why I write...that is how I fight. I can't stop talking about what happened to me until something is done about it. I am an activist for myself right now, because who is going to fight harder for me than me? My life is an open book now, and eventually I'm telling it all. Eventually I'm going to tell how I, a level headed, intelligent woman, who just happens to be a counselor, who was married for 14 years, and who typically makes great decisions in love and life, could end up in this situation. I will not be bound by what happened to me because I did not deserve it and I did nothing to cause it. I have no shame, guilt, or embarrassment...why should I? I'm the one that got hurt, so all of that belongs to him. What I do own in all of this is not listening to my inner voice. We are disloyal to ourselves when trust others more than we trust our own spirit.

I am tired of crying – it is time for me to fight back.

Thursday February 6, 2014

I just went to my first face to face therapy session today in all these months. For months, I have talked to my counseling colleagues by phone, I have done brief phone counseling, and I have tried to counsel myself, but today was the first day that I got real therapy, and I needed it. I think I found the right therapist. Dr. Kola is skilled and highly educated, but very compassionate, spiritual, and intuitive. I prayed for the right person to walk me through this because this situation is not for the faint-of-heart, and not every therapist is equipped to handle this level of trauma. I thought that I would prefer a woman, but I think having a man will be better. He will be the objective one that I'm going to allow to walk me through this journey, the one whose emotions I don't have to worry about, so I can cry when needed. Everyone needs help sometimes, even a professional helper like me. I'm glad I stopped procrastinating, being too picky and ridiculous, and finally went to therapy. Let the healing begin…

Friday February 7, 2014

Dr. Kola became a little emotional as I told him my story yesterday; I thought that it was because he felt sorry for me, so I apologized for causing him distress. He said to me, "It is not your job to rescue me. You can't be the counselor now Christy." He told me that he needed to feel what I feel because the moment he couldn't feel a client's pain is the moment he shouldn't be counseling any longer. He went on to say, "My tears are because I truly believe that I am witnessing a real life angel." He said that he had never seen anyone hurt and transformed so badly and in such an evil way but yet still radiate so much power, love, and faith in God. He said that my presence overwhelmed him and evoked emotion. He was curious about my lack of hate or bitterness for Drew because he has seen clients hate for far less. He wondered how that could be. I told him I don't know, because I don't. I don't know why I don't hate the man who destroyed my life. I am angry, but I am not consumed with hate and bitterness.

Saturday February 8, 2014

As I approach the one year mark of my tragedy, there has been no obvious change in my life, but strangely I feel a shift in the atmosphere, I feel God moving things around, I feel Him working things out. As I said, I finally went to therapy this week, which was a move in the right direction. After therapy, I stopped by my mom's house and guess what was waiting for me? A package in the mail from my childhood friend, Deidra Freeman. Deidra sent me a beautiful yellow scarf; she'd heard me mention that I needed scarfs to cover my scars, so she sent me one. I cried because every time someone performs an unexpected act of kindness towards me I attribute it to God's grace and favor in my life. I think this is why I do not allow myself to hate or focus on the negative too long. Hating would make a mockery of something incredible, and that something incredible is the innate goodness in most people. In spite of it all, the good outweighs the bad. Evil is the minority, so why should I give it focus? Evil has no power over me, not even the power to make me hate it.

Monday February 10, 2014

I went out to a crowded restaurant for lunch today for the first time since before the attack. My brother and I met with my foundation's new marketing and technical team, and then we met with the staff at the Georgia Coalition Against Domestic Violence. It was an eventful day. I went out, talked, and acted the way I have always acted when doing business. I held my head high. I did not focus too much on the stares of strangers or how I would affect others. Today I advocated for myself. Today my voice was heard. Today I felt normal. Today I felt empowered. Today I felt free. Today I felt like *me*.

I think a lot. I am an introspective chick. I just figured out why I will not allow myself to be consumed with hatred. It is for the same reason that I was leaving that relationship...the same reason that I prefer entrepreneurship...and for the same reason I have never once tried addictive drugs...not once. I do not like my mind or my body being controlled by any person, place, substance, or thing. I do not hate simply because it is expected of me. I will not hate because hate consumes you, controls you, zaps all of your positive energy. It would dim the light inside of me, and I don't want that for myself. I don't hate simply because I don't want to. I control me; no one and nothing else does...just me and God.

"I Will Win"

I think God is about to elevate me...
To a level that I can't yet imagine
I'm still in the midst of the storm...
but the tide is turning and
I'm feeling a bit more calm
I can't see it all clearly now...
but I know I'll finish this fight...and
I believe that I'll win somehow.

Thursday February 13, 2014

Hmmm, it just occurred to me that I have stopped crying every day. Nothing has changed, so I guess that I'm just all cried out for the moment. I am no longer pretty...I have accepted that. I cannot work right now...I have accepted that. Life will never be the same again...I am beginning to accept that. I have to have my entire face replaced and will look like a completely different person; it will take me some more time to accept that one. I don't think that I will ever accept that he did this intentionally and is still free. There is no play book for this one.

Self-awareness is a beautiful thing. I just realized something about myself that I have always done. Whenever I'm going through something heavy like right now, I limit my own grief so that I don't cause those around me additional grief and discomfort. As I approach this one-year mark in April, I feel like I should be moving forward and approaching acceptance, and that others are ready to move forward. So I say that I'm okay, but if I don't let this flow and take its course, I know that I will suffer and grieve for years just as I did when I lost my daughter. Everyone moved forward, so I pretended to move forward to make them okay and comfortable, as I suffered in silence. Right after her passing, I started a new business, I ran the Peachtree Road Race for the first time, I lost 30 lbs. I did everything possible to try to move forward and appear okay. I think I grieve the way that men typically do...by getting busy – hence my taking all of these new things on like the foundation, speaking publically, and telling myself that I have accepted this. I've made progress, but this is still some bullshizz...this is not okay, I am not okay yet, I haven't accepted anything, and I'm still grieving...there I said it. This is me finally taking care of me and my own psyche and emotions. I am having a breakthrough. I will be just fine, but I'm not there yet...

Saturday February 15, 2014

Elon is turning 11 on Tuesday and typically I would plan a sleepover or a girl's day out with her friends, but this year I cannot participate because I cannot be around her friends. They can't even come to the house. In fact, my kids can't have company at the house anymore at all because my appearance would definitely be disturbing to other children, especially those that knew me before. So her dad is going to take her and a few friends to Sky Zone, which she will enjoy, but I still want to do something special for her, something simple, but from me...something that will overshadow all of this craziness. I have finally stopped trying to protect my kids from everything because it is impossible, but I want them to have some good memories of this time and age, mixed in with the bad ones.

The universe is at work again. I've been looking for my copy of *Seat of the Soul* by Gary Zukav all week because it is time for me to read it again. Some books are so heavy and enlightening that you have to read them again as you grow and gain more understanding and life experiences, and this is one of those books. I read it years ago, and I got it then, but my spirit has developed so much that I'm certain I will discover even more this second time reading it. I mention all this because guess what had come in the mail when got home? Yes, a brand new copy of *Seat of the Soul,* shipped to me from one of Machon's friends. This was not even one of my friends, and I never mentioned that I was looking for the book. The universe is amazing, and knowledge comes to us when we are ready to receive it. In my opinion, this is one of the best books written about spirituality and consciousness, but you have to be ready for it or it will go right over your head. If you truly "get it" you will never be the same again. Your level of consciousness will change, and you will see life differently. The only books that have affected my level of thinking more are *Courageous Souls* and the Bible.

Wednesday February 19, 2014

Quinn finally found a job in Atlanta and will be in town full-time. My brother is my protector, my friend, my daddy at times, and my child at times. Sometimes I'm his big little sister and have to keep him in line, but I adore him all of the time. His name is Anthony Quinn, and he's the one who taught me how to win. He taught me about boys, he hid my toys, he aggravated me by sucking on my fat cheeks. He fought bullies for me, and he lifts me up when I feel weak.

He taught me how to drive, how to save money, how to be both gangsta and princess at the same time. He still holds my hand when we cross the street the same way he did when I was 4 years old, if truth be told. He taught me work ethic and how to not just survive, but to thrive, how to be "from" the hood, but not be "of" the hood. He taught me at 16 that "I am the master of my fate, and the captain of my soul." These words are worth far more than gold. He was the first in our family to ever go to college, and he is the reason I became a "Master" just before my disaster.

We are both flawed and perfectly imperfect, but we love each other, and I know that he always has my back. In fact, if he could, he'd carry this burden for me — I know he would. My big bro is back in the "A," and I'm feeling okay.

Thursday February 20, 2014

Because of the loss of my outside appearance, I am forced to spend more time on the "inside," literally and figuratively. I cannot wear my make-up or adorn myself with jewelry. I have no need for hot curlers to style my hair because the doctors cut it all off and it's still growing back. There is no need for me to wear my pretty clothes or high heeled shoes. No, my outside cannot be my focus right now, so I focus on the inside. I focus on adorning my spirit, enhancing my soul, sharpening and expanding my mind, further developing my character, and purifying my heart. Yes, that is my focus, and maybe that is the purpose of it all — to make my heart a work of art. Hopefully one day my outside will again mirror my inside because pretty on the inside is nice, but pretty on the outside was fun and lovely too. I want it all...

95

Friday February 21, 2014

"If by day I honor God and treat His people right, then I can rest easily and sleep peacefully at night."

I believe that the ability to graciously say "no" when saying "yes" does not benefit you is one of the keys to happiness. Saying "no" requires no explanation because things understood don't need to be explained. There is a big difference between being selfish and being self-centered. Being selfish is simply to have a heightened interest in one's own well-being. It is necessary to be selfish in order to be happy at times because if you do not fill your own cup first, you will not have what is necessary to pour into other people. I have learned the value of a little selfishness and I can take care of myself and others, respectively. There are times when I have to put myself even before my kids because if I fall, then we all fall and I cannot let that happen. By contrast, self-centered people only take care of themselves, because they view themselves as the center of the universe. That is the difference, so be a little selfish when it is necessary, and just say "no" when saying "yes" is to your detriment. Trust me, you will be a lot happier and a lot less resentful. Saying "no" when I needed to would have changed the course of my entire life.

Saturday February 22, 2014

There is a lady in the UK who was attacked by sulfuric acid the same way and for the same reason that I was back in 2008. She was a beautiful young model named Katie Piper who was planning to end a relationship, and a guy poured a coffee cup full of acid all over her face. For months I have used her story for information and inspiration because of how she was able to overcome her struggle. Thanks to my dear friends LaNese Harris and Stanley Nelson contacting Katie on my behalf, she and I have been communicating by email. Katie's entire face was burned and disfigured just like mine, and her entire face had to be replaced just as mine does. She looks like a different person now after 60 surgeries, but I think that she is actually more beautiful now, so there is hope for me too. She is sending me a copy of her book, "It Gets Better," and I have been looking for it in the mail daily because I need to see someone who has gone through exactly what I'm going through...I need to see them on the other side of it. I need hope. Katie is pregnant now; she is in love. She has a successful talk show, and a foundation. She is modeling again, and leading an extraordinary life. Katie gives me hope for a normal life. To God be the glory. I wrote her this message the other day: "Katie, my dear; your pain was not in vain because as I go through this pain, you are my inspiration. Once I get through this I will reach back to someone else, the way that you are reaching back to help me now." Once you make it through any kind of hell in life, it is a must that you go back to that hell sometimes, to pull another out of their hell because that was likely the purpose of it all. Katie's ex-boyfriend is now serving 15 years in prison. He is now in bondage, and she is finally free. One day, that will be me.

Sunday February 23, 2014

Another way to get through something challenging or horrific in life, other than talking about it, is to find reasons to be grateful through it. Some mornings it is hard for me to even get up and face another day, so what I do as soon as I wake up, before I have to look at myself in the mirror is I find several things to be grateful for. I have to do it before the devil can get to me through doubt and depression, discomfort and weariness. I stop him in his tracks by thanking God for the things that I do have like a comfortable home, a supportive family, my eye sight, the use of my hands and legs, no extreme pain, my children, my incredible friends, kind strangers, good doctors, a large window next to my bed so that I can be awakened by the light of the sun, pretty feet and hands, a nice shape to my body (I'm burned, but I'm still fine, and yep, I even thank Him for silly little stuff). I'm grateful for food, lights, water, heat, my ex-husband and his family, and for life. This attitude of gratitude is how I am able to keep facing my days. If I waited until good times to rejoice and be thankful then I could be waiting a lifetime because as long as we live, the challenges will keep coming, so I choose to do it now, right here where I am. If you can read this, then you have something for which to be grateful.

Monday February 24, 2014

53 more days until my first facial reconstruction surgery, the replacement of my cheeks. Every 2 months after, another part of my face will be replaced. I also have 64 more days until the 1 year mark of this happening to me. I will

also have to officially resign from my job as a counselor in April too, so I'm feeling some type of way this year about spring coming. I'm not sure yet what that type of way it is, but it's definitely not my normal spring fever.

When I finally get through this phase of my life, I really want to start back traveling. The past year has taught me that the only things important in this life are the people that you love and the memories that you make with those that you love because you can't take anything else with you when you die. You cannot take your money, your cars, or your houses; you can take absolutely nothing but love and memories. I'm going to find a way to take my kids and my mom to every place that I've been planning to visit like South Africa, Tuscany, Amsterdam, Hawaii, Canada, and Japan. I'm taking that Alaskan cruise that I've been planning on for years. I'm going to start back skiing, something that I use to do every year, but I haven't done in forever. I want to learn to play the piano, and learn to fly a small plane. I can't wait to start running again and start back running road races, but I'm mostly excited about being able to see my kids play sports again; being a baseball and soccer mom is looking really good right about now. The good thing about getting a second chance at life is creating sweeter memories. Everything will be sweeter and richer than before, I hope...

Wednesday February 26, 2014

As I prepare to face the grand jury soon, I've been forcing myself to relive that fateful day because I know that I will have to give an accurate account of it again, and it's been 10 months. I just forced myself to listen to the 911 call on Youtube. I have only been able to listen to it a few times, but every time I listen to that call I hear something new that I did not catch before. Just now I could hear him clearly lying and complaining about how badly *he* was burning, when 20 percent of my body, including my face was covered with acid, and he was barely burned. He said that he was rinsing me when he never did. He said we fell, when we did not. I just heard him saying we were fixing the toilet, when you don't put drain cleaner in a toilet because it is for the drain, and there was nothing wrong with anything in my house. Hearing 911 tell him to rinse me off 6 different times made me cringe because every time he put the phone down he would come back and force me back down to keep me from water. As I listened to my own screams of agony, I got really angry all over again, but some anger is necessary. I needed to revisit that day because things have been too silent. I'm ready to fight....and fight...and fight. I am kind, and I deserved better.

My feelings were hurt after listening to that 911 call earlier today. I haven't cried in a while, but I cried for two hours. I cried until my nose turned red like Bozo the Clown, but then I turned my frown upside down by giving my entire house a redesign, and I did not spend a dime. It looks like a totally different house. I love change, and typically I change my hair style, my wardrobe, my man (kidding), and my house just in time for spring. I change everything. But this year I just changed my house...oh, I'll be changing my face soon as well...ha.

Thursday February 27, 2014

Katie Piper's book came in the mail today. I have so many books to finish reading, but I must read this one first. I need it right now. This is how God works; we receive exactly what we need when we need it. I am ready to look at the other side of this hell now finally, so guess what her book is about? Yep – making it to the other side of this horrific journey, surviving and thriving after having your life stolen from you. Thank you, God...You are indeed the best of knowers.

Tomorrow is the 10-month mark and some incredible milestones happened today. First, I ran into my dear old friend, Carol Jones. This is a big deal because only a few people have seen me face to face. I don't know why God put Carol on my path today at the doctor's office, but I felt compelled to speak with her and acknowledge her, in spite of how bad I look. I could have kept walking because she didn't recognize me, I am unrecognizable. But the God in me said, "Say hello to your sweet friend and trust the God in her, and let her feel whatever she needs to feel in this moment...it will be okay." So I spoke to her and we hugged and she cried, and I had to walk away before I cried because I reached my cry quota for the week yesterday after hearing the 911 call again. Seeing her was emotional, but I think that it was necessary for her and for me. The second milestone was me driving a car for the first time since April 27th of last year. This is a really big deal because I was told 10 months ago that I would be legally blind and never be able to drive again. They were wrong. I cannot be all over town just yet, but just being able to drive up the street felt normal. I felt like me again. I felt like the realtor, the mom, and the counselor that I was, not burned and helpless and weak. Seeing my friend and driving again were really big deals. Today was a good and courageous day.

Friday February 28, 2014

It is 10 months today since my life went astray and I am still here and only slightly cray-cray. My therapist brought out some relevant points yesterday, and although therapy is private and sacred, the conversation was broad enough for me to share some stuff. He explained why I might have felt compelled to redesign my home after hearing the 911 call and crying for hours. His take was that just like as in my writing, grief and pain sparks my creativity and decorating is also a way that I show my creativity. Also, hearing the tape angered me and reminded me that this man took my home, my safe haven and made it feel unsafe for me and my children, so the act of changing everything around me was my way of taking my home back, since moving is not an option right now. He also reminded me of something that I know to be true and that is a recurring theme in my journey: I am a spiritual being having a human experience. My keen awareness of my "spirit" and the God in me is what makes this tolerable for me. My understanding of the temporary and the illusion of this burned and disfigured body, and the "knowing" that this is only a moment in time and it is a critical part of my life lesson is what makes me who I am. My strength is in my awareness of things unseen, things that are unlimited, things that require faith. He also said that the gravity of my tragedy is likely sparking the humanity in everyone around me, and that is why people are so connected to me and this story. Having a different perspective is nice, and being a counselor in counseling is interesting...

Saturday March 1, 2014

I am feeling better physically this week than I have in a very long time. This is the longest period of time that I have had between surgeries and my energy level has been strangely high, so I'm trying to do as much as I can before my 10th surgery in April. The "face off" is what I call it. I've been tending to my nest all week, trying to make our home feel warm and cozy again for my baby birds. I missed spring cleaning last year because my season was cut short, so I'm clearing my space and getting the kids organized so that things run smoothly in my absence. Today felt like a normal Saturday, and I did normal things. I used to bore easily and deplore normal and mundane things, but now normalcy is the best thing ever. After lying in a hospital bed for 3 months and being away from my kids for 6 months, me just being able to watch TV with them, clean my own home, walk outside, and decorate is like going to Six Flags. I am grateful for these bits of normalcy because I know that God is in every bit of it...

Monday March 3, 2014

I decided to never call myself ugly again no matter how awful I look because I have never once in my life called another person ugly, not once. My grandmother taught me at four years old to never use that word to describe one of God's children; so why would I use it to describe myself? I am transformed because of someone else, and how could I be more kind to others than I am to myself? I am no longer that pretty girl that I once was, but I am still God's child and too beautiful on the inside to ever be called ugly, even jokingly by me. Yes, I miss my beaming smile, my dimples, my freckles, and scar free skin. I likely won't have them again. But I am not ugly...I am beautiful within.

What the what?! My surgeon, Dr. Spence, just said, "Oh...I forgot to tell you that after this next surgery, in order for the skin graft to take, you will not be able to move your mouth at all for two weeks...that means no eating or talking at all. WTH? Really, God? Really? I feel like I'm being tested for sure. Am I on candid camera, because this is a bit much for one person. Now I've got to starve and be quiet too? I've got to sip through a straw for two weeks...seriously? I guess I'll be losing more weight. I got it God, you think I'm strong and you know I can handle this. But seriously? You know how much I love food, it is my best friend. Are you preparing me to do missionary work in starving countries or what? You must be preparing me for something extraordinary. Wow, no food for two weeks.

Lord help me, I'm about to venture out and start driving my truck again. Machon will have my truck up and running again tomorrow. I thank God for this ex-husband of mine. My truck has been just sitting in my garage for nearly a year. I'm tired of waiting on folks to do things for me. I'm out of here tomorrow. I have no money and I don't know where I'm going, but

I'm hopping in Big Bertha and rolling up out of here somewhere tomorrow, so clear the road because I'm breaking free...

Tuesday March 4, 2014

My decisions are so much better when I'm "quick to listen, and slow to speak," and when I follow my intuition. I have heard my inner voice my entire life, but I ignored it at times when it could have changed the course of my life. Intelligent people listen more than they speak because you learn more this way, about life and about people. If you pay attention, the most simple minded people are loud and running their mouths all the time, never really learning anything. Just pay attention the next time you're in a crowd of people...I bet I'm right.

Wednesday March 5, 2014

I've been waiting for April 17, 2014, the date of my facial reconstruction since I woke up and saw my face for the first time in June of last year. What in the world will I look like after surgery? How will I ease into this new face, this new skin? How will it feel? Will it be sufficient for what I have remaining to do in this life time? How will my children adjust to yet another me? Only God knows. "I'm off to see the Wizard, the Wonderful Wizard of Oz..."and he's gonna give me a new face. Ha.

I'm showing my face soon, I think. It's been a year, I think it is time. I needed time to get use this, and for my kids to adjust some before I started exposing myself completely. But drastic times require drastic measures, and what is the point of going through all of this if something does not change drastically as a result of what happened to me? I'm going to pray a little bit more, but I am no longer concerned about being exploited, and it is not possible to embarrass me, not even in this state. Embarrassment has never been my issue because I know who I am and Whose I am. My greatest concern has been my children. If I had shown my full face months ago, this would have likely been on every channel and on every show because my change is just that drastic. I actually turned down a talk show interview a few weeks ago because I didn't think that format would be good for me. I don't have a need to be seen just to be seen, and I have no interest in being well-known, but I do have an interest in saving and changing lives. My suffering, my family's heartache and my life will not be in vain. I will not let that happen. Unveiling soon...I think.

I'm showing my face soon I think. It's been a year, I think it is time. I needed time to get use this, and for my kids to adjust some before I started exposing myself completely. But drastic things require drastic measures and what is the point of going through all of this if something does not change drastically as a result of what happened to me? I'm going to pray a little bit more, but no longer concerned about being exploited and it is not possible to embarrass me, not even in this state. Embarrassment has never been my issue because I know who I am and Whose I am. My greatest concern has been my children. If I had shown my full face months ago this would have likely been on every channel and on every show because my change is just that drastic. I actually turned down a talk show interview a few weeks ago because I didn't think that format would be good for me. I don't have a need to be seen, just to be seen, and I have no interest in being well-known. But, I do have an interest in saving and changing lives. My suffering, my family's heartache and my life will not be in vain. I will not let that happen. Unveiling soon...I think.

Friday March 7, 2014

Prophet # 1

Inger has been telling me about a prophet that she met recently and how much she has been helping her. I am a spiritual person, and I believe that some people have the gift prophesy, but I am very leery of false prophets because everything and everyone is not of God. Still, I have grown to trust Inger and I trust her spiritual insight.

Inger and I arrived at Prophetess Iantha Taylor office's in Douglasville Georgia at 11 am. We sat in her well decorated lobby area and waited. We could hear her praying with someone behind closed doors. Actually, she was doing more than praying; she seemed to be passionately worshiping and the loud noises gave me a bit of a pause, but I grew up in the Baptist church, so I am accustomed to this sort of thing. As I sat there, a spirit of peace came over me. I began to anticipate her telling me good news about my future.

After a few minutes, Iantha came out to greet us. She hugged us both and directed us toward her office. We walked in and sat down. I sat in a large plush chair and Inger sat directly in front of me in a folding chair as Iantha remained standing. We all held hands and Iantha began to pray fervently. As she prayed, I began to fill up with so much emotion that I could not contain myself. I could feel the presence of God in that room and I was assured by the Holy Spirit that this woman was indeed a prophet and a woman of God.

Iantha said that my story would heal and bless millions of people throughout the world. She said that I would become a powerful public speaker. She said that lives would be saved and transformed. She told me to do something with my hair to regain some of my femininity. She said that I was about to be in front of a lot of people, and even with the scars it is important that I feel as confident and as much like my old self as possible. Iantha said that I would write several books and that my words would be so powerful and impactful that people from around the world would quote them. I enjoyed hearing all of this, because it gave me hope and meaning, but it all sounded so far-fetched. I have never spoken in front of large crowd, and I don't feel anywhere near presentable enough to be in front of people. As Iantha was praying and consulting with God and giving me instruction, Inger sat there praying silently and holding my hand. I knew that Inger and I would become close friends the moment that I received her letter a few months ago, but I had no idea just how important she would become to me. I love her, and I can see how genuinely she wants to help me.

Iantha gave me so much hope and a renewed sense of meaning and purpose. She ended by asking me if an old male friend had come back into my life and I told her about my cocoa butter friend, the one who I speak with almost daily. She closed her eyes and said, "I don't think he is the one that I am seeing. He is needed in your life now, but an old acquaintance will re-enter your life within the next two years and he will change your life forever. I don't believe that this current friend will be here much longer." I was puzzled, but I received it and we left her office.

Sunday March 9, 2014

Happiness is not a word that I would use to describe this phase in my life. The last time that I felt truly happy was on April 28, 2013 at about 2 pm. I had bliss that day. The beaming light inside of me blinded him in the midst of his darkness so he tried to put my light out. He failed because a beam of light is even more brilliant when it is surrounded by darkness. I have learned to cope through humor and jest. I am being sustained by the love of God, and the love of family and friends. I am slowly taking bits of my life back. I am being resourceful and focusing on what I have instead of what I do not have. I don't have my looks anymore, but thank God that was never my greatest asset. Now my real assets are needed like my intelligence, my humor, my writing ability, my genuine nature, my graciousness, my survival skills, my positive thinking, my critical and strategic thinking, my counseling skills, my marketing skills, my spiritual insight, my defiant nature, my competitive nature (I don't like to lose at anything so he can't win). I am not happy; I am just learning to cope. I am angry to the max every day.

My anger is what wakes me up when I really want to lay in bed in the fetal position and cry all day. My anger is why I keep talking and writing when I really just want to climb into a rabbit hole and hide. My anger is why I am allowing myself to be vulnerable, and soon I will show my disfigured and unrecognizable face to the world. I am foiling his plans to destroy me, weaken me, isolate me, make me unloved and unwanted. He would love it if I hated him because hate is just as strong as love. Well, I am not letting him have it. You will never see me bashing him, you will not see me ranting and raving publicly. I will not be that angry black woman. I have punched quite a few walls in my house, but I will not let him win. He would win if my true nature changed in addition to my outer looks. So, no I am not happy or okay. I am just a defiant pint sized 5'2, 140-pound woman, with a 10-gallon heart, a 50-gallon spirit, and an infinite soul that cannot be broken.

Monday March 10, 2014

People often ask me how I can remain gracious in spite of what has been done to me. The simple answer is I am gracious because I am surrounded by grace. Something very evil happened to me, but it does not define me. I don't know why I was allowed to go through this, but I have not been alone. God sends me a new angel every single day to help me get through this. That is why I remain gracious...and grateful.

Today I am thankful for my angel, Machon. We have lived here together since I came home in November, and he came to me yesterday and asked if I was strong enough for him to leave and go back to his home now. Anxiety rose inside of me as I thought of him leaving and me having to go back to doing everything on my own in this condition. He drives me absolutely nuts at times, but I have so much love and adoration for this man. I often watch him sleep on the couch after he has worked all day, after he has injected my weekly saline shot into my abdomen, after he has taken Chris to baseball practice and Elon to tumbling class, and I am just filled with so much gratitude. I knew that he would have to leave and go back to his house soon, I just hope that I can give the kids what they need. I still don't leave the house without a veil and sunglasses. This will be challenging, but I want him to resume his life; I want him to be happy. I want him to find a nice, beautiful, and strong woman that will love both him and our children. He deserves happiness. I will miss the security and comfort that his being in the house with us has given us, but I love him enough to let him go. God is with me, so I will be fine.

I have mastered the art of taking meditative trips. I am imaging myself in a house at the beach, decorated with all white decor like Diane Keaton's house in the movie *Something Gotta Give*. I want to sit and write all day and then take long walks and collect white seashells for my white and pristine beach house. That is my dream...to live in a house by the sea...and just be.

Wednesday March 12, 2014

There are many forms of control and abuse. I honestly didn't know that I was in a cycle of abuse because he was so romantic and accommodating for the most part. "I love you" ten times a day. Flowers. Cards. Candy. The works. But it did not *feel* right, and still I always wanted to leave. I was always running because I always felt controlled and manipulated, and suffocated. In retrospect, he had all of the characteristics of a sociopath. They are skilled at getting what they want by identifying other people's voids and filling them. They are the most charming and charismatic people on the planet by definition. They are typically marvelous in public, but monsters in private. Not all are dangerous, but most are sinister and can't feel remorse or empathy, hence being able to watch a person burn alive and not be affected. I assessed mental capacity for a living, but I faltered in this assessment because it was personal. I am not ashamed of the truth; it has set me free and allowed me to be me again. I could be wrong, but I believe that I dated a sociopath.

Thursday March 13, 2014

How many people know what it's like to go from beauty to beast in one life time? How it feels to be burned alive, to have your clothes eaten through, and to be burned down to your bones, down to the nerves...and know that someone planned and watched this? How it feels to be in a semiconscious state for two months? How it feels to only have a few areas left on your body that have not been touched or scarred, because even what was not burned is now scarred from being used to graft the areas that were burned? How it feels to have to re-learn how to use your arms and legs because you were laying so long? How it feels to have your eyes sewn shut, and when you finally wake up, still not be able to see or talk because you are blind and have a tube in your throat? How it feels to have the skin from your stomach sewn on to graft your face and neck? How it feels to wear a tight leather coat as skin that covers your entire face, arms, neck, chest, and shoulders? How it feels to look in the mirror and not recognize yourself? How it feels to go through all of this and not have justice? How it feels to face the person for the first time and see no remorse? How it feels to see your own child and frighten her so much that she can't see you again for months? How it feels to live in isolation? How it feels to be invisible

107

and live behind a veil? How it feels to see people you know and they not recognize you? How it feels to be raising your children in the midst of it all, but not be able to be seen with them in public yet? How it feels to still find bits of joy in the middle of hell? How it feels to be able to see God even in the mess? How it feels to go from counselor to client? How it feels to be planning a graduation at 2 pm, and burned alive by 2:30 pm? How it feels to face evil eye to eye? How it feels to know that you have been with a sociopath? How it feels to prepare for unveiling yourself to the world? How many know what it feels like to go from successful and independent, to nearly disabled and totally dependent on others for finances? How it feels to not know what you will look like in a year? How many people know how this feels?

My only crime was ending a relationship...

Friday March 14, 2014

I had a moment at Brewster's tonight while getting ice cream. Elon went to get the ice cream and I stayed in the car. She came back with the tiniest scoop of ice cream for me that I have ever seen, so of course I'm pissed cause I haven't had my chocolate turtle ice cream in a year, and I was looking forward to stuffing my face. I felt cheated, and mama don't like being cheated. So I told her to go back and get more ice cream because that tiny scoop was ridiculous (it really was, and I'm not just being hoggish). She didn't want to go because she hates conflict and being embarrassed. But I kind of like conflict and can't be embarrassed, so I went to the window, past the people in line, while Elon stood at the car looking mortified and I asked for more ice cream. The girl said that the ice cream shop now had new scoops sizes. I said, "Are you telling me that your prices have gone up, but your scoops have gone down...really? Look, I'm gonna need more ice cream, baby, and I really don't have time to argue with you because we're missing "Dance Moms." She looked at my burned and crazy-looking face, paused for a moment, and then went and brought me so much ice cream that I couldn't finish it. I got back to the car and Ms. Scary Pants says, "Really mom? What did you say? Did you show out? You're acting like your old self. Wow, you're the only person that will come out of hiding and show out for a scoop of ice cream." Moral of the story? Don't try to punk me, and don't play with my friggin' food.

Saturday March 15, 2014

I'm feeling "in the hallway" today. I am in the middle of test and testimony. I am at a crossroads. Should I go left or should I go right? Should I keep going straight or should I just stand still for bit? Doubt means don't so I'm standing still for a bit. This Godly wisdom is some kind of wonderful. It is very different from the worldly wisdom I had before. I am mastering the art of staying calm in the midst of the storm and remaining peaceful during chaos. There is a hurricane circling around me, but I am still standing. I will remain unmoved; even as things and people fly to and fro, I will remain unmoved. I am still standing...

Prophet #2

For months my mom has been telling me about her friend Jannette Watson who is a pastor and a prophetess like Iantha Taylor, the lady I saw with Inger a few weeks ago. Mom has been trying to get me to meet with Pastor Jannette for several months, but I wasn't interested. However, after meeting with Iantha a few weeks ago and receiving hope, I decided to finally meet with this prophet.

Mom and I drove to Jannette's home which is just five minute from mom's house. Her home was clean and pristine with tasteful décor. She led us into her redesigned garage area that she repurposed for worship service and we sat down at a round table. Jannette sat in front of me and mom sat next to me and just as Iantha had done, she began to pray as mom and I prayed silently and held hands. Jannette opened her eyes and said to me, "You are one of God's chosen and He is so proud of you." She went on to confirm everything that Iantha had prophesied a few weeks ago, so now I have confirmation, but Jannette added something that I truly needed to hear in that moment. She told me not to wait to help people...to do public speaking. She said that God would heal me over time, but I only have a short timeframe to get my message out, and that it is pivotal that I do the work as I heal. She said that my scars would heal other people, and that they would look at me and not only see my true beauty, but the beauty within themselves through me. She said I will always have scars, but I will be beautiful in spite of them and one day I will wake up and they will no longer be a problem. God will not restore me to my former self, but He will renew me. Just as Iantha had done, Jannette encouraged me to finish my first book as quickly as possible because that book would be the catalyst for many more. She said that writing would solve a lot of my financial problems. She said that Drew was possessed by a demon and his mission was to destroy all of my senses, to affect my mouth, my eyes, my ears, and my nose, but God would not allow him to kill me. She said there was an evil presence there that day, but God was also there. Strangely, Iantha also said that there was a divine spirit there with me that day. I felt it then and I believe this with all my heart. After meeting with Jannette, I am more certain about revealing my face on TV, and also excited about receiving my Fortitude award in person. I am no longer afraid; the work must be done now with the scars.

Sunday March 16, 2014

I have decided not to change the way that I love people. I love hard and endlessly, with intensity and purpose, and not just men...people period. No, I will not change that about myself. I will instead be more particular about who I decide to love. I will be sure that in the future, I will choose as T.D. Jakes says, a 10-gallon lover like myself because a person with only one pint to give would never fill up my 10-gallon tank; it is impossible. This applies to all relationships, not just romantic ones. A person can only love you to the level of their capacity to love, period. And if they don't love themselves first, then loving you is truly an impossibility. My number one lover for quite some time shall be me. I'm loving myself hard and endlessly, with intensity and purpose because I need it most right now, and no one deserves more love from me than me. My tank is running on empty right now. I must fill it up so that I will be able to pour into others when needed. In the words of Shakespeare, "To thine own self be true." I am loving me first and foremost.

Monday March 17, 2014

I wonder why we are often more kind, accepting, nonjudgmental, and nurturing to others than we are to ourselves. If a friend or mate gains, weight we encourage and uplift them, but if we are overweight we beat ourselves up and punish ourselves. We will forgive others sometimes faster than we will ever forgive ourselves for mistakes. I would ask my substance abuse clients these questions: Would you give your children or anyone that you love poison? Would you allow your child to put drugs like meth that are made from household chemicals in his or her body? Their response was typically, "Of course not!" or "Hell no Ms. Christy!" My second question was...So why would you poison yourself or put drugs in your body? Do you love them more than you love yourself? This was typically a lightbulb moment. It forces a person to look at how we truly feel about ourselves. Who in this world could be more important to you than you? Your life party doesn't get started until *you* arrive. You are the star of your own movie; other folks are just co-stars and extras. You are the common denominator in your equation. People will come and go, but at the end of your life there will be just you, so take care of you first and most. This is not selfishness or self-centeredness; it is simply self-love.

Tuesday March 18, 2014

My interview this morning on WAOK went pretty well, I believe. I also prerecorded an interview with Ryan Cameron and Wanda Smith at V-103 that will likely air in the morning. I'm not sure why the story seems to be getting more attention than before. It could be because I'm out of the house now and can actually see and hear people's reactions. Several people stopped me today just to hug me and say hello. One lady said that she had just gotten out of an abusive relationship because of my story (this is why I can't stop talking). I kept Elon with me today and let her experience my interviews, and I let her see me on TV yesterday for the first time. I realized that my trying to shield and protect my kids and isolate them so much from this horrible thing was also confusing them because their friends come back and tell them so much stuff. She was dreading going to school today because she feared what the kids might say about my TV interview last night. I also realized that it was making them feel alienated from me. I wanted my daughter to see me being strong and positive and to see other people's reaction to me. I think that hearing me speak about the Delta's Fortitude Award today empowered her and made her see another side to this story, and another side to her mommy.

Friday March 28, 2014

I wish that I had the wisdom and insight to start the Christy Sims Foundation without having to go through so much suffering, but I have said it before – pain births our goals and our talents, and it takes us out of our comfort zone. I'm guessing that if I had not had to endure so much, I would not have had the courage to help myself and others. This foundation is comprised of such a diverse and incredible group of people. I'm so excited about what we are about to do that I wish I didn't have all these surgeries coming up. Taking the focus off my problems and focusing on how I can help others after I have rebuilt my life is aiding in my healing. Our suffering is never just for us.

Starting this domestic violence foundation is just me doing what I do best: turning sour, rotten lemons into sweet southern homemade lemonade. Absolutely everything that he took from me, every pain, every scar that I have will be used for my good and for the good of others. Just watch God work this out...just watch. Watch how many people gain as a result of my pain. I don't know the how, when, where, who, or what, but I know God.

Monday March 31, 2014

I just read something interesting on one of Chris' T-shirts. The shirt said "Choose your life; don't let your life choose you." I have lived by this philosophy my entire life without even thinking about it. I planned my life as well as I could. I planned my education, my career, my children, my marriage, I even planned and designed my home, but what happens when you choose your life, but it flips on you and doesn't choose you back? What happens when life smacks you in the face? What then?

Being in a crisis is an interesting place to be for me. I'm in crisis mode and when in crisis, you have no time for nonsense, no time for inauthenticity, or pretentiousness. You have no time to sweat small stuff. My focus is on those things that insure my mental and physical survival. I can only check for folks who are checking for me. My focus is on those that I love the most. In a crisis, you have no time for mistakes, so all of my decisions are God driven and based on my intuition, yet strategic. The beauty of being in a crisis is you discover who you truly are and what you are capable of. You discover who your real friends are, and some are weeded out as new ones come in. The friends with you in the valley are friends indeed; the rest are just associates. Crisis, if handled with mostly your spiritual self and not solely your human self, can cause more growth, enlightenment, love, awareness, humanity, compassion, and spiritual development than you could have ever achieved if life remained peachy. Crisis is necessary because it encompasses our pain and pain births our goals and our talents. If you have not survived at least one major crisis in your life, then you likely have not reached your highest and best potential. Crisis is simply training for greatness, I believe.

Wednesday April 2, 2014

As far as days go, this one was okay. I interviewed with Tracye Hutchins at CBS Channel 46, then I hung out with my mom, which was cool. I love that as I have grown into a woman, my mom has become more and more my best friend. I love her and I really like her too. After I dropped my mom off, I went grocery shopping for the first time by myself, which was interesting. I got lots of stares; some people recognized me from the news, and some I'm sure wondered what the heck happened to that poor soul, but as always I just kept walking and minding my own business. Tomorrow I'm taping a reveal special with Lisa Rayam of FOX 5 News that will air in May, so look out cause here comes Christy Boo Boo and who knows, it's getting hot out so I may just wear a halter top or something so folks can see what is really going on with me. Yep, I'm showing it all, no sunglasses and no head gear. It's not pretty, but it is me for now. I have to do it now because my face is about to change and it's been a year almost, and this life of bondage that I have been living is simply not conducive to my spirit or my personality. It is time for me to set myself free.

The moment that we have all been waiting for finally came last week. I testified for the grand jury to bring charges against Drew a few days ago, and it was one of the hardest things that I have ever done. My mom, my brother, and I sat on a wooden bench outside of the grand jury room for what felt like an eternity. We arrived at the Henry County Courthouse earlier that morning with the expectation that I would testify early. However, as the hours passed, we wondered what was happening and why was it taking so long? There were no other witnesses; could Sandi Rivers and the investigator, Kip Jarrard have hours of evidence to present to the jury? Was this a good sign? The three of us sat and prayed, and tried to joke at times because that's what us Three Musketeers do when we feel pressure: we find a way to laugh our way through any situation.

Finally, after hours of waiting I was called into the grand jury room, and before taking the witness stand I was sworn in by the ADA, Sandi Rivers. This was only my second time being in any type of courtroom. After being sworn in, I sat down and tried to calm myself down. My heart was racing as I sat there in front of 21 grand jurors. They all studied me with their eyes as Sandi began questioning me about the day of the assault. It has been nearly an entire year, but surprisingly, I remembered every detail of that day up until everything went black in the ambulance. I remembered that entire morning as if it had just happened. I sat there on the stand as if I were on trial. I felt alone and afraid as I faced the grand jury of 21 men and women. They seemed horrified and shocked by my scars. Some of them were unable to look directly at me, some of them searched my face for the truth, and some of them shed tears along with me as I wept out loud. I had not cried in weeks, but they asked me questions about my children, and about the horrible pain that I had endured and it forced me to relive every moment of the past year leading up to this point. Sitting there in front of all those people baring every scar was agonizing for me, but it was necessary. Through my tears, I bravely and boldly spoke my truth. I can only hope that my words and Sandi's evidence were enough for an indictment. He has been walking free too long, and as long as he is free, I am not safe. I hope they felt my pain – I hope that my words and my scars were enough.

Thursday April 3, 2014

Well, two more hurdles jumped. I testified for the grand jury last week, and today I unveiled my entire face on FOX 5 News with Lisa Rayam. She reported my story a few months ago, and I felt comfortable with her so I wanted her to be the reporter to reveal my face to the public for the first time. This is a monumental day for me, and I'm not sure how this will affect me or my family. Every interview that I have done so far has been in shadow or behind a veil, but I felt it was time that people see what he did to me before I have my face reconstructed. My greatest fear has been causing my family and my children embarrassment. My face is disturbing, but how will people ever truly understand if I don't show my face? I was right to choose Lisa because she handled my unveiling graciously and professionally. Instead of interviewing in the studio, just the two of us interviewed in a dimly lit private room surrounded by only the camera man, my mom, and Bunnie Jackson Randsom. We just sat and talked, and once again I shared my truth. The interview will not air until next month, but it is done. I did what I have been dreading for months. I unveiled my burned and severely disfigured face, and now I just have to pray that it has the desired effect. Now I just have to wait and see what happens next. I have been walking in my Courageous Christy role as of late, and it is both terrifying and liberating...

I am exhausted, mentally, physically, emotionally, and also spiritually. I've been in spiritual warfare and it is tiresome, but I cannot stop...no time to weep...To quote Robert Frost, I have "miles to go before I sleep...and promises to keep." I'm moving forward.

Saturday April 5, 2014

My spirit has been calm today because I have been operating more in the now. Anxiety resides in two zones, the past and the future. We are typically regretful about something that happened in the past, or anxious and worried about something that we anticipate in the future, when we can control neither. However, when we focus on the moment, allowing ourselves to be fully present in even the simple things (like sitting on the floor playing jacks with the kids), we have less anxiety. Yesterday is no more, tomorrow will take care of itself, and the things that we are most fearful of will likely never happen anyway, and if and when

115

they do happen, we will survive it, just as we survived that last big thing because God is with us now, just as He was with us then.

Monday April 7, 2014

It may sound strange, but I prayed for Drew's soul this morning. I did not pray for Drew, the man, because I'm just not that good of a person yet. As far as I'm concerned the man can kick rocks and play in traffic. I prayed for his soul because it is eternal and I can't even imagine what my Heavenly Father has in store for this soul. Lord, have mercy upon his soul.

I am letting go and letting God. I testified for the grand jury, I cried for 30 minutes, I prayed for a while, then I went home and I haven't worried or thought about it much since. I do these interviews and I think about them an hour before and maybe an hour after, and then I go home and I take care of my kids and go on with my life. This is how I am surviving: minute by minute, letting God handle the stuff that is too hard and too heavy for little ole me. A strange peace has come over me, and it is hard to articulate. I believe that greater is coming.

Wednesday April 9, 2014

I look horrible, but I think that I shall take myself to dinner and a movie today. I am slowly unleashing and removing the chains that have had me bound for nearly a year. I have decided that when April 28th arrives, I will not dwell on it and remember it as the day that my life was destroyed. Instead I will view it as the day that God gave me a second chance to live and a new purpose for living. I will have had surgery and have my new cheeks by then and I think that I shall skip right on over to April 29th because it is a new day and a new year and I am moving forward. This challenging midpoint is possible to bear because I have survived the horrifying beginning, and I can visualize the glorious ending.

I speak often of the movie, *The Shawshank Redemption* because it is my favorite movie, and I liken my proverbial prison to Andy's literal prison, but this week I am feeling more like my man Red (Morgan Freeman). I am marking my name on the wall – "Christy was here, but now she is gone," and this Saturday as I receive the Delta's Fortitude Award, I will see my family and friends again. I will hug them and shake their hands just as Red did with Andy on that beautiful beach at the end. It has been a long time coming. This will be my first public event since my tragedy, and I am nervous, but "I'm so excited that I can barely sit still or hold a thought in my head. I think it is the excitement only a free man can feel, a free man at the start of a long journey whose conclusion is uncertain. I hope I can make it across the border. I hope to see my friend, and shake his hand. I hope the Pacific is as blue as it has been in my dreams. I hope." Oh how I love this movie…

Saturday April 12, 2014

I am full, I am loved, I am blessed, I am free. I felt beautiful today. I felt like me today. I felt joy today. I have never seen so much beauty and love and courage in one room in all of my life. I walked into a sea of red, into a crowded room of more than 500 hundred people, I walked in behind the mothers of the slain Trayvon Martin and Jordan Davis, women that I have watched on TV, prayed for, and admired, but the roar of the crowd was not for them, it was for me. They were cheering for *me*; they were proud of *me*. They are honoring me for being bold and consistent and mentally strong. Those that I love most in this world were with me. Not only was this my first time in public again, but Chris and Elon were there with me. My mom and dad were there. Mr. Sperling and Maria, whom I adore, were there. This day was so special and so healing for me. People that I have not seen in 30 years were there to see me receive this award. After all of these months of her counseling me and helping me by phone, I finally saw Dr. Cherry Collier face-to-face. She has been such a blessing to me. I felt so special.

It was such a pleasure meeting Sybrina Fulton and Lucy McBath, both lovely women. Today was powerful. Today, once again I released the chains that have had me bound because I showed my burned and disfigured face in front of a crowded room filled with many people that I did not know and some that knew me before when I was pretty. This was yet another milestone on my journey. I felt honored, humbled, and blessed to receive the Delta Sigma Theta Fortitude Award. I am so thankful that my childhood friend, Desiree Robinson nominated me, and I am glad that I postponed my surgery in Baltimore so that I could experience this. If I had not gone to receive the award in person, he would have won another victory over me, over my life. I could not let that happen. I was cloaked in my Courageous Christy cape today. Today was a good day.

Monday April 14, 2014

I've been waiting a year for my burns to mature enough for Dr. Spence to reconstruct my face, but it's nearly time to leave and I'm in no way prepared to go. I have to recover in Baltimore for an entire month and I haven't even packed. I do this procrastination thing right before every surgery. Why? Because I'm scared, I don't want to leave my babies for weeks, I'm feeling good and surgery makes me feel bad, I don't like lying in bed for days, I don't like being cut on, and I know that I will look awful before I start looking better. I believe that it will all work out because this is my 10th surgery and God has not failed me thus far, so He won't fail me now, but it is not every day that a person has their face removed. I am human, and honestly, I'm terrified!

Tuesday April 15, 2014

On April 10th, my brother Quinn's birthday, the Henry County grand jury indicted Andrew Lee Fordham, Jr. on four counts: one count of aggravated assault, two counts of aggravated battery (one for disfiguring me, and one for causing me blindness temporarily), one count of burglary for entering my home after the incident and taking items from my home. Yes, all of this because I was ending a relationship. I chose poorly and I have paid for it dearly. I stayed in that relationship longer than I wanted, and I was even with him that weekend to spare his feelings. I denied my own feelings...I will never do that again. I am relieved to have this part of the process done before my surgery. It was important to me that the grand jury see the damage that he caused me prior to my first facial surgery this Thursday, and God worked that out for me. It is too soon to rejoice because we still have to go to trial and he has to be convicted, and rejoicing over something like this is really not my style, but I will say it once again, "unearned suffering is redemptive," and God's timing is not our timing. God does not play with folks who mess with his kids. No amount of jail time can make up for what Drew has done to me and my family, but it is good to finally see my case moving in the right direction.

Wednesday April 16, 2014

Sleep didn't happen for me last night. I couldn't get my brain to shut down. Not only did I not lay down, I didn't even sit down all night. I've been prowling around here like a freaking vampire all night. I'm headed to Baltimore today to have the surgery that will be the beginning of the new me. I have anticipatory anxiety I suppose, but I need sleep, and now daybreak has come. I'm about to send my baby bears off to school and I won't see them for almost a month. "I'm off to see the wizard...the wonderful wizard of Oz." I'm going to get a new face, ha!

Mom and I made it to Baltimore, and Lisa Rayam and her camera man from FOX 5 are here with me at the hospital. I feel kind of special. They flew here from Atlanta to capture my surgery and to meet Dr. Spence.

Guess who else is in Baltimore with me? My two best friends, Jonell and Lanese. Lanese always has my back when I'm here, but Jonell flew in and surprised me...and boy did I need it. I need all the support I can get for the face-off tomorrow.

11:15 pm

OMG...I only have 45 more minutes to stuff my face with food. I think I have more anxiety about not being able to eat after 12 than I do about them taking the skin off of my face...I think that would classify me as a foody and maybe even a little hoggish, but I must stop writing and go eat because I only have 37 more minutes. After surgery my jaw will be wired shut for the next two weeks, so this is my last chance to pig out...

Sunday April 20, 2014

Surgery #10, part one of the face-off, is complete. My face is literally sewn on. Dr. Spence grafted donor skin onto my cheeks Thursday to prepare my body to receive my own skin perfectly tomorrow. It is so freaky and weird, but kind of amazing. Burn reconstruction is a delicate medical specialty, and it is very different from plastic surgery. Only a few surgeons in the world can do this, and Dr. Spence is one of the best. People travel from all over the world to have surgery with this brilliant man.

I pray that I'm ready for surgery tomorrow. I've been having some complications that I'm concerned about; my face is not responding well to the donor skin. I am swollen and in terrible pain, and I look like a monster. God help me...

Monday April 21, 2014

The face off, part 2, commences at noon. Last Thursday Dr. Spence removed all the skin from both my cheeks and replaced it with donor skin, which is basically a dead person's skin. This was necessary in order to prepare my body to receive my own skin. This is a very delicate process because donor skin can only last 4 days before my body realizes that it's not my own skin and starts to reject it. It was necessary to use donor skin first because the skin on my body is so limited and he needed to increase the chances of my body quickly receiving my skin grafts – there are no do-overs with this. Today he will remove the tissue expander from my right abdomen and use the extra skin on my stomach to replace the temporary donor skin on my cheeks. He will discard the donor skin, just ask he did my scarred skin last week. Because the cells of my body have already been tricked and the tissues have already started preparing to receive skin in the site, it is expected that my own skin will now adhere easily. I know it's strange and kind of creepy, but it is also medically wonderful too, don't ya think?

Of course, to increase the chances of the skin graft being successful, my mouth will be wired shut for the next three weeks as I recover at the hotel. I will only be able to eat through a straw.

I imagine that I look as bad right now as I did last April, maybe worse. I have two large yellow bandages on each cheek. My face is swollen and distorted; I look like a monster. I am unrecognizable again, and so tired of these folks asking me what happened, especially since I can barely move my mouth and talk. I just point to my mom, and she explains. You know that you are bad off when a doctor is almost brought to tears when looking at you, but this is a part of the process. I can stop the process and just stay burned and disfigured – some burn survivors actually elect to do that, but that's not who I am. I want to be and look the best that I can, even if there is pain.

...

I'm so thankful for my mom. This powerful and praying woman of God loves and hovers over me so much that she drives me a little nuts at times.

She does not leave my side when I am in need. She takes every trip to Baltimore with me. When I'm in the hospital, she sleeps in the bed right beside me. Nurses come in trying to take her vitals and stuff because she is laying in a bed just like me...lol. When I'm in surgery, she is in the waiting room interceding in prayer on my behalf. The interesting thing is, my mom has never been the mother hen, hovering kind of mom. When I have my own strength, she stands back, and she never gets in my business. She has always allowed me to be free and independent, even as a young girl. I have actually always kind of watched over her in a way, because she is so easy going. But when Satan came in and stole her baby girl's life, my quiet and shy mama got mad and became this mighty warrior, my greatest advocate, and my very best friend. My mama rose to this challenge like a warrior. I am so glad that she lives, and that she had me so young because she is still healthy to be a 43-year old's mom. I love this chick right here, and of course, she is sitting in the bed right next to me...talking about some silly stuff (I got my silliness from her) and laughing at herself because my mouth is wired shut, and I cannot talk or laugh with her. As usual, before she falls asleep, she will randomly break out into some gospel song and completely destroy it because she cannot hold a single note, but she loves to sing...and I will sit quietly and let her because I love her, and because I have no choice. I can only shake my head. I want to laugh, but I can't! My mouth is wired shut! Hmmm, I think she secretly likes that my mouth is wired shut and I can't talk. I am being held hostage by this silly, tone-deaf, gospel singing woman over here. God help me, please!

I have not spoken to Chris and Elon since I left home and it's tearing away at my heart. These surgeries are necessary, but I feel like I'm always abandoning them. I know that Machon and Connie are taking great care of them, but I am their mother. The pain pills are not working, I am in agony, the wires in my mouth are killing me and I'm hungry as hell. Depression has set in again. I hope they have him in jail until his bond hearing. This is so hard, but it would be harder if he were not indicted. Thank God for that.

Sunday April 27, 2014

Joel Osteen is talking about that "internal warning sign" that I speak of often. I ignored my internal sensor, and thus here I am. It is real, and if it

121

doesn't feel right, then it is not right...it is the Holy Spirit tugging at you. Remember, we are made of mind, body, and spirit. Our spirit is what protects us from evil, from the unknown. Please don't make my mistake and ignore the most powerful part of your being. If you don't have peace about anything in life that you do before you do it, then you won't have peace after it...even if it looks, feels, or sounds good, it is likely not good for you. Let peace be your umpire. Doubt means don't. That uneasy feeling is God tapping you on your shoulder, warning you. You may not realize it, but that day that you were late and frustrated...and just couldn't get it together...and the Spirit told you to change outfits at the last minute or go back home...you may have missed a fatal accident that day, and instead of being stuck in traffic, you could have been the cause of that traffic if you had left 20 minute earlier. That is how the Spirit works. It is not always the big things; it is often the little decisions that save us.

I have been trying not talk about it, complain about, or think about having my mouth wired shut, because it had to been done for these skin grafts to take, but I am hungry as hell! I have not had solid food since 11:52 on April 16th, the night before my first surgery. I have been burned, scarred, grafted, sewn up, cut on, and shaved bald. I was in a coma for two months, away from my children for months, and without justice for a year. I wear a mask and compression garments 20 hours a day, I look like a freak, I lost my job, my money, my freedom to come and go, I had to learn to walk again after coma, I was blind for 4 months, and so many more things that I have survived and never talk about, but dammit, this liquid diet is the last straw. I'm about to crack up. I AM HUNGRY! I just dreamt of ribs, mac and cheese, collard greens, corn bread, yams, and banana pudding...and it was orgasmic. Two more days, two more days, two more days. I pray that I don't go crazy and rip these wires out before Tuesday.

Monday April 28, 2014

It is April 28th, and one year ago today my life was forever changed. I made it. I made it through the most horrific year of my life. One year ago, Andrew Lee Fordham Jr. threw acid in my face and turned my life upside down.

I try to avoid the details of that day as much as possible, but now that he has been indicted and I know for certain that I will have to testify against him at trial, I have made it a point to remember as many details as possible. I drafted this letter to Sandi Rivers a few months ago while it was still fresh in my mind:

Sandi,

This is a lot of information, and none of it may be helpful, but it is the absolute truth. My life and my appearance have been forever changed, my children have been traumatized, and as long as this man is free, I do not feel safe. I hope you have enough to charge him.

Andrew Fordham and I dated for a few years, yet the last two years were the most committed and intense. We were discussing marriage during the year prior to the assault. He was very charming and romantic at times; however, I began to have doubts because he was becoming increasingly manipulative, jealous, possessive, and controlling after I began my work as a counselor at an all-male substance abuse program. He questioned my every move. He went through my phone and my computer without my knowledge, and would then drill me later about the contents. I would describe our relationship as co-dependent and sometimes volatile. Our biggest issues were my kids not liking him and his jealousy and control. His greatest fear was me ending the relationship; he hated being left. I left the relationship several times due to his controlling behavior, and he would call excessively and often camp outside of my house until I talked to him. I cared for him, so I always went back.

In September 2012, we had a disagreement at his home in Sandy Springs, and I wanted to leave, but before I could get to the door, he pushed me to the floor and stood over me yelling. He then hid my keys so I could not leave. I spent the night there and went home when he calmed down the next day. Once again, he begged and apologized, and I went back to him after a week or two (my biggest mistake). I stayed in the relationship, but I was never the same, and I became increasingly more disenchanted and distrusting of him. In the months prior to incident, we were talking less and seeing each other only two weekends a month when my kids were away. I did not allow him around my kids anymore because my son said that he felt a siren go off inside of him whenever Drew was around, as if we were in danger. Drew complained constantly that I was backing away from him. I told my family and my kids that I was ending the relationship, however I

123

felt that I needed to handle him with care because his father had just passed, and he had already become aggressive in the past when I tried to leave, so I did not know how he would respond to an abrupt breakup. We barely saw each other, so I thought that I had time and that slowly backing away would work better…I was wrong.

On Tuesday April 23rd, I mentioned to Drew that the drain was clogged in my hall bath. He offered to fix it when he came for the weekend. I said that I would try to remove any debris myself and that I had Drain-O under the cabinet. I fixed the drain on Wednesday April 24th and told Drew. My kids and I took showers in that tub several days prior to the incident, as it was not clogged. Drew used the shower that Friday and Saturday without any issues. He arrived at my house on Friday April 26th, and we spent the evening together. We got up Saturday morning and both showered before leaving the house. I spent the afternoon at a baby shower, and he stayed at my house alone. We spent Saturday evening together. We got up Sunday April 28th, the day of assault, and I showered in that same bath without issue and was dressed by 11 am. I spent the afternoon addressing my graduation announcements while he watched TV. I finished a conversation with my mom at approximately 2 pm, then went into the kitchen. Minutes later, he yelled out to me to bring him a towel. As I approached the bathroom, I stopped in the hallway. I was puzzled by the enormous amount of water on the floor because I had walked past minutes before and there was no water.

There was no water in tub, none in sink, and the toilet was not overflowing. I questioned where the water came from and why he was holding a bowl of fluid. He stood there in nothing but shorts, holding the bowl with both hands. He never answered, but looked at me strangely and step towards me and doused me with the liquid. I had no idea what the liquid was, but my eyes began to burn so I ran to the sink to rinse my face. I stopped rinsing and yelled at him, "What was that? Call 911 and ask them what to do!", and he just stood and watched me for a moment. Prior to dousing me, he was sliding in the puddle of water by the tub. He expected me to enter the bathroom, but because I never came into the bathroom and was standing on carpet, he had to step out of water towards me to douse me. He never slipped and fell as he reported, and I was standing upright and still on the carpet outside of bathroom. Splatter on the carpet and walls in my hall prove how far away from him I was as he came towards me. If he had fallen, he would have damaged himself and probably would have dropped and broken the ceramic bowl, and my entire face and upper torso would not have been completely covered if he had fallen. He never fell. It happened so fast, and although he was complaining all weekend about me being distant and less attentive, we were not arguing so I did not know I was in any danger. I did not know what was in the bowl, and I did not react fast enough to get out of the way. I did not know he was supposedly "fixing" the tub or toilet because neither were clogged, and I never saw him bring the chemical into my home. I never saw the bottle of Clean Shot. He brought the chemical and the bowl into the bathroom without my knowledge, and put the water on the floor. There is no other way that much water could be on the floor in a matter of minutes. It was too much for a towel to pick up. He told my family that the water was there because I had just showered. That was a lie. I showered 3 hours earlier and left no water on the floor, and if I had, this amount was way too much to come from getting out of a shower. I never leave water on the floor, ever, because it drives me nuts.

I went to the hall and sat on the floor as he called 911 because I could no longer see; I was completely blinded by chemical. I could not hear his conversation, but he kept putting the phone down and coming back to stand over me. I kept trying to get up, but he kept holding me back down. I begged him to rinse me off because I could feel my skin burning off, and I was in agony. He said "they said not to rinse you off because it will ignite chemical, just sit here." I kept screaming at him, "I hate you, I hate you…I will never be the same!" The EMT finally arrived and asked him why he had not rinsed me, and he said because the phone ranged. They told him to get in shower and get dressed, but they stripped my clothing and took me outside to rinse me with rain water. My last memory is telling Drew to call my mom and my ex-husband. He kept yelling that it was an accident. All I could think of was my children being on their way home, and his two kids being alone at home. I have no memory after the ambulance ride. I heard that I told a detective and a nurse that it was an accident, but I have no memory of saying that or anything after the ambulance ride. I would imagine that I would say that it was an accident because I did not know exactly what the chemical was, and I would not expect him to hurt me to that extent, but Drew grew up in Miami with people that are from countries where acid attacks are common. He kept asking my mom about my face after the assault. I am not certain that he wanted to kill me, but I am certain that he wanted to make me ugly, and this was the best way.

He told my mom that the bowl was up high and I walked by and it fell on me. He told my ex-husband that the container was a coffee cup, and that he fell flat on his face and the chemical got on me. He told Det. Brand that we had made love all morning, when we had not. He lies a lot. I believe that he is a sociopath….he showed no remorse when I faced him in court.

One last thing. I have a very protective poodle who barks and tries to protect me when I am in danger. I believe that he put my poodle up prior to the incident. Sam would have been right at my side barking and would have been heard on the 911 tape if he were loose. He planned this. He has eight aliases in five different states and his extensive criminal record proves that he has a criminal mind and is capable of planning this.

Questions:

1. Would you go purchase industrial grade drain cleaner containing 93% sulfuric acid to fix a drain that was not clogged?

2. Would you buy the chemical and bring it into another person's home without even telling them?

3. If you thought the drain was clogged, wouldn't you use the Drain-O under the cabinet before buying sulfuric acid.

4. Would you take a cereal bowl from a person's kitchen without their knowledge and put sulfuric acid in it without even asking them if you can use bowl?

5. Would you ever in a million years pour sulfuric acid, which is used to melt metal, out of its container and put it in a cereal bowl?

6. Would you stand in a puddle of water holding a bowl full of dangerous chemical with two hands, wearing no gloves, no shoes, no shirt, nothing but shorts?

7. Would you tell 911 that you were "fixing" the toilet, yet tell the police

and everyone else that it was the shower, if you were telling the truth?

8. Would you let a person burn in agony after you were told by 911 and begged by the person to rinse them off? He never rinsed me off, and would not let me get up to rinse off, yet he testified under oath at the TPO hearing that he rinsed me off. My brother, Anthony Tucker, testified at that same hearing that Drew gave him the same answer about the chemical igniting when asked why I was not rinsed. If I had been rinsed, I would not be permanently disfigured. I had no idea that it was sulfuric acid in the bowl until I awakened from coma two months later, nor did I know that 911 had advised him to rinse me. When the ambulance arrived, they also questioned why he did not rinse me. If I had been rinsed, my clothes would have been soaked. I was burned down to my bones and within 2 cm of my heart, and this would not have happened if I were rinsed.

9. Would you tell the person that 911 said that you could not rinse her off because water would ignite chemical, when they never said that?

10. If you slipped and fell wouldn't the chemical get on you since you were not wearing a shirt, instead of completely covering the other person's (me, who was fully dressed) entire face, chest, neck, and arms? He got 3 small spots on him, yet I am burned over 20% of my body and completely disfigured, and have minimal use of my left arm because I was burned down to my nerves.

11. Would you tell 911 that the chemical was burning through your clothes if you were only wearing shorts, yet not mention that the chemical was burning through my clothes down to my bones? 911 asked him directly if he was rinsing me with soap and water, and he said yes on the recording. HE NEVER RINSED ME…he was lying even on the 911 tape.

12. Would you leave a woman that you supposedly loved in the emergency room not knowing if she would live or die and rush back to her home to clean up all the evidence, leaving the hospital knowing that police wanted to question you?

13. Would you steal the person's jewelry, laptop, and iPad just after burning her alive, if it were an accident and you had remorse? He had borrowed $1200 dollars from me the previous month and never paid me back. I am

guessing that he needed money and stole from me in order to pawn items.

14. If you were the police, would you question the victim while she is in shock, burned severely, and heavily sedated, yet wait two weeks to question the abuser, giving him time to concoct a story?

I appreciate your efforts in my case. Thank you so much for your compassion. I will call you next week.

Christy Sims

Tuesday May 6, 2014

Mom and I flew back to Atlanta a few days ago, but I can't go home to the kids until I heal a bit more. I am looking horrible after this cheek surgery, nearly as bad as in the beginning. I don't want them to see me like this.

I was asked this question: How do you do it, how do keep waking up and going on? This was my answer: I don't do it, the Holy Spirit that dwells within me does it for me. This reminds of the day my daughter Kayla passed away 12 years ago and how I thought I would never survive that, but I did. How I thought I would not recover from divorce, but I did. How I thought I would never get over all of the many losses I have suffered, but I did. How I didn't know how I would get through all those sleepless nights and long work days during grad school, but I did. It reminds me of the day last year when I was near death and thought I would never see my children again, but I did. It reminds me of lying in a coma for two months motionless, voiceless, and sightless, and not knowing if I would awaken, but I did. How I woke up and wondered if I would ever walk or see again, but I did both. It reminded me of just three weeks ago when I thought I would not survive two surgeries in one week, but I did and I'm back home recovering. I did not know my own strength.

Wednesday May 7, 2014

The week prior to the attack, he called my cell phone 25 times back to back to find out where I was because it was after 8 pm and I was not home. I was waiting on Elon to get her hair done, and had left my phone in the car to charge for just an hour. Now this was not my husband, not my fiancé, and we didn't live together. I questioned why he had called so many times back to back like that, and how possessive that was...after first accusing me of cheating...and then lying and saying that he had only called 5 times. His response was that he was worried sick about me, so I let it go...again.

Thursday May 8, 2014

I am in love with my children. How do I know? Because they are my first thought when I open my eyes in the morning...and the last thought when I close them at night. I'm ready to go home and be called mommy a zillion times a day, and wash a billion clothes, and say "leave her alone" 10 times, and hear "I'm hungry" non-stop...and watch reruns of "iCarly" and everything else on Nick and Disney, and scrub baseball pants until my hands get tired, and try to do homework that I never learned and don't understand, and answer a billion questions from her, and ask him 100 questions trying to figure out what's in his 14 year old brain, and try to make them feel safe in a world that is not safe, and try to maintain my sanity, and fall asleep at 1 am only to get up at 5:30 am and start it all over again. On second thought, maybe I'll just stay at my mom's and be her baby a few more days. I don't think I'm quite well enough yet...

Friday May 9, 2014

I am so unpretty that it is laughable. But you know what my cocoa butter friend said to me last night? He said, if this is your worst after having acid thrown in your face, then how blessed you are, because there are some folks who have never been hurt, and can still only dream to be as beautiful as you are right now, after being attacked by acid. Your worst is someone else's best. He said, "think about it CJ...a chemical that is used to cut through metal and steel covered your entire face and upper body, and it still did not completely destroy you...something that destroys metal and steel, didn't destroy *you*. I can still see you." Something to think about. I guess I really am a "steel magnolia."

Saturday May 10, 2014

My inspiration today is my 11 year old daughter, Elon Marie. Why? Because she is taller and bigger than any 11 year old girl you will ever see. In fact, she is bigger than me, but she is one of the sassiest, baddest gymnast you will ever see. My chubby little girl has more confidence than some super models, and can do anything that a skinny girl can do. My big/little girl has stage presence and personality, and she can flip, tumble, do back hand springs, walk overs, round offs, splits, and cart wheels like nobody's business, but I just spoke with her on the phone, and she's a little nervous because she's trying out for competitive cheerleading today, and she's hoping that her size doesn't hinder her, that the judges look beyond her size and see her ability. My words to my daughter were, "You are beautiful. You are just the size that you need to be right now, and you are worthy because you have prepared for this for 4 years. There is nothing that you can't do…a little anxiety is good so use it. I will be there with you in my heart and in my spirit. I love you, Elon, I am so proud of you for trying and doing your very best. Your best is good enough; *you* are good enough." I can't be there with her today so I hope that my words were enough. God, please send love and light to my baby today at 1:30, the time of her tryouts. I'm missing so much…deep sigh.

Tuesday May 13, 2014

It's time to leave mom's house and go home. I'm not quite healed the way I would like to be, but I haven't seen my babies in a month…too long. I may have to just put a bag on my head so I don't freak them out. The skin from my stomach is now on my face…just imagine what that looks like right now. Going home…it's been too long.

There is nothing like my own bed after being away for a month. I have one month at home, then it's back to Baltimore for my next surgery in June, then July, and hopefully I won't have to go anymore after August. Dr. Spence is retiring in June after 40 years as a surgeon, and he is coming back just to finish my burn reconstruction. I am his last patient, so I can't waste any time. This process will take 2-3 years or more from my life, and time away from my kids, but I'm thankful that although I will never be the same, I will get much better, and there is hope for a better life. When I'm done paying for this medical stuff and can sustain myself, then my real work will began: helping other survivors. My life is now purpose driven. I never knew how that felt until now. I am driven by my pain…and the pain that I feel for so many others. I can't escape it, I can't see my reflection in the mirror without being compelled to fight back, and not just fight for me. I was already doing meaningful work before, I was saving lives as a drug, HIV, and mental health counselor, but this is different. Every person that I prevent from harm by sharing my story will be like me healing apart of myself. That is powerful…that is purposeful. That is the *why*. There should always be a *why* to what you do. We suffer then survive so that we can then share, save, and heal – that is the purpose. If you have made it through something and have not reached back, then you may have missed the point of it all. I'm still in the middle, and I have not made it through yet, but when I do, watch out.

Thursday May 15, 2014

The "Face for the Faceless" special which is airing tonight on FOX 5 Atlanta will be my last TV interview for a while because I will be in reconstruction and recovery mode for many months. I prayed and decided to show my entire face prior to starting my facial reconstruction because I felt that it would be important and possibly life saving for people to see the full damage that was done before I started improving. I hope that it was a good decision and I hope that it doesn't cause my kids too much embarrassment or any harm. My kids have to deal with this stuff at school. I have been hiding all this time to protect them, but I can't hide any longer. I heard that the special will be real, raw, and compelling. I hope it helps someone, because it was hard for me to do this.

I'm missing my nephew, Anthony's graduation right now…and it's pissing me off. Eight kids in my family that I absolutely adore are graduating this month, and I will miss them all because I am recovering from something that I did not cause. I attend everything; showing up is what I do (I'm usually late, but always there). I am annoyed. I'm missing memories, and let's not get started on all of my kid's stuff that I'm missing. It annoys me that Drew spent only a few hours in jail. He bailed out the same day he was arrested a month ago. He is still free, and that makes me angry. Jay walkers spend more time in jail than that. I'm pissed, you don't get do overs with some things like a childhood or a high school graduation.

Friday May 16, 2014

I don't know how I got the nerve to put myself on TV looking so horrible. I am a pretty girl to my core. I don't even like going to the mailbox looking crazy. This desire to look my best is not derived from vanity, it is derived from the pride within myself that was instilled in me by all the pretty and proud women that raised me. I decided to do this unveil special because something within me said to do it now before I improve. I have been in bondage for a year, and revealing myself will hopefully free me and may save someone else as well. I called Lisa Rayam and said "I'm ready, I'm ready to show my face to the world. It is time." It was hard to watch, and I cried like I was watching someone else's sad news story, except it was mine. My kids are so over this stuff that they didn't want to watch, so I sat alone and watched it and wept for my own sad little self. I feel somewhat relieved to have it done, so I can move forward. It is the last interview I did before my change. I have changed again since that interview, and I have no clue what the final result will be, but it has got to get better. Strangely, not one kid said anything crazy to my kids about their burned mama being on the news, so I guess they are becoming accustomed to seeing me now.

Monday May 19, 2014

I have experienced every emotion imaginable. In one year, I have experienced feeling loved, hated, desired, controlled, possessed, smothered, burned, blinded, paralyzed, immobilized, weakened, humbled, isolated, alone, admired, strengthened, blessed, adored, publicized, angered, exposed, betrayed, nurtured, encouraged, inspired, uplifted, depressed, rebuilt, accepted, bound, and finally freed. I have lived a life time and gone from beauty to beast to beauty in one year. I fought death and the devil and beat them both, and I became better acquainted with the God in me.

I was extremely comfortable within my own skin, and he was extremely uncomfortable in his, so he destroyed my skin to even the playing field. The dysfunctional mind is indeed a black box.

Wednesday May 21, 2014

People in other countries have seen my face now. A lady named Bridget contacted me from Ireland yesterday, she said that she had seen my story in an international blog. Yep, I'm out now, but I still can't go to my kids' school or let their friends see me. They are still embarrassed by me. I thank God that I am a counselor and understand child development and I am not hypersensitive, otherwise I would be in a ball of tears. Elon has said, "Yes, I'm proud of you and yes I know you're courageous and everyone has seen you, but have you forgotten what it's like to be eleven? Kids my age are not all compassionate and I don't want to be questioned about you all day at school, so please don't take me to school." Then she said, "I'm just trying to survive my last few days of 5th grade." My kids didn't ask for this, so for a little while I will operate in a way that is most comfortable for them, but not much longer. It is time for us all to be released from this bondage.

Saturday May 24, 2014

I'm about to venture out and buy some flowers to plant. This is my first time out in public here since the last surgery, and I'm still a bit pieced together and not quite right, but I want to do some yard stuff so I'm going. Drew hated for me to go anywhere that men might be, like Home Depot, gas stations, repair shops, car washes, and my all-male job. He would literally try to drive across town to pump my gas to keep me away from gas stations. He said it was in the name of chivalry. We would argue about me washing my own car at the car wash. No worries about me being picked up anymore; he has made sure of that. I can't imagine any man finding me attractive now.

Abuse is not always about someone hitting you physically. Sometimes they can hit your soul by making you feel caged and unfree. I am no longer a pretty woman, but at least I am mentally free. Both men and women can be controlling, sometimes women more often than men. Me sharing my story is not always to help those who might be abused, I also share to give the abuser a mirror so that they can stop it.

It's Memorial Day and as usual I am alone. I just passed by a house that had the smell of ribs coming all the way down the street. I wanted to crash that party so bad! I was so tempted to walk up to the door and say, "Hey, I'm Christy Sims, you know the burned lady from the news. Do you mind if I get a plate please?" I'm thinking that at least one person would have recognized me, and said, "Sure come on in Christy, eat all you want and come back tomorrow and Monday too! Don't even think about cooking; in fact, bring your kids too!" I was tempted, but I kept driving and came home. Then five minutes after I got home, guess who comes by with a plate full of food for me from a cookout he had just left? Machon. If this man does nothing else, he's gonna feed me. The universe is spectacular. I must not be all bad if the man that I have been divorced from for six years is still concerned about my well-being.

I am feeling some type of way about Maya Angelou's passing. It is not sadness because I know that she lived a long and incredible life, and she lived it on her own terms. What I feel is a sense of loss of one of the most peaceful, insightful, intuitive, wise, and artistic people that has ever lived. She was not just a poet and a writer, she was first a professional dancer and performer. She screamed creativity and she is definitely one of my writing influences. She was what we in the counseling profession refer to as self-actualized, which means to reach your highest and best potential as a human being. Only a few people ever do this before they die. A phenomenal woman has transitioned. R.I.P. Maya Angelou.

My favorite Maya Angelou quote...

"One isn't necessarily born with courage, but one is born with potential. Without courage, we cannot practice any other virtue with consistency. We can't be kind, true, merciful, generous, or honest."

Wednesday May 28, 2014

I have finally recovered enough to go back to therapy tomorrow. I know some people are ashamed of going to therapy, but I am a therapist who needs therapy and I am not ashamed. I love myself enough to get help when I need it, and I am honest enough to admit it. I have had a lot going on and I am unloading tomorrow. I hope Dr. is Kola ready for me. He will need all of his skills, knowledge, and experience to handle me tomorrow. I am a hot mess.

Thursday May 29, 2014

One of my dimples is back. I just noticed a few minutes ago that after this last surgery I now have a faint dimple in my left cheek. Even Dr. Spence was surprised when I told him. I noticed it because I smiled really hard today and it was there. It is not as deep as before, but it is there. I thought my dimples were gone forever. My face is more narrow now, but I can still see my high cheek bones. It is the little things, even the tiniest amount of progress, gives me hope and display evidence of God's healing power.

Friday May 30, 2014

There is a distinct difference when that woman-child of mine, Elon, is not home. The house is calm with just Chris and me. We just look at each other and enjoy the silence. When Elon is in the house, you know it, but Chris and I can sit in total silence and be okay with that. My son and I are kindred spirits. No words are required – we just know that we love each other. He knows me probably better than anyone else. Our spirits are both calm and peaceful. We have the same random and dry humor. We are both mentalist, introspective, and insightful. I love him as my son, but I really like him as a person too. I pray that he will one day find a woman of God who will love him as much as I do. He tells me every day that he loves me and that I am beautiful. He prays for me more than I pray for myself...this is a 14 year old that I'm speaking of, so get ready world.

Monday June 2, 2014

I have a few things that I still like about my physical appearance, so I think I'll highlight them as much as possible. I still have really cute and tiny hands and feet with no scars. My legs from my knees down are still nearly flawless. My smile has changed, but I still have nice white teeth and this one faint dimple in my left cheek when I smile hard. My stomach is scarred from surgery, but my stomach and waist are as flat and tight as a 10-year old again after this last surgery. I still have a sexy curve to my body for a 43-year old woman who has carried three babies. My hair is short and no longer relaxed, but I will rock this short curly look and make it sexy. It is not about vanity, it is about me being a woman and still needing to feel like one. Pretty is not just a look – it is a feeling, and every woman wants to feel pretty in some way. I am focusing on what I still have. I don't have my pretty face, so I will keep my pretty hands and feet polished and wear cute sandals. I will wear dresses that highlight my pretty legs and my shapely figure. I love me enough to highlight my strengths, because this is for me and not for anyone else. I love myself at any size and in any skin. I have healthy self-esteem.

Saturday June 7, 2014

I have been going through old pictures of myself because I realized in therapy the other day that I gave myself a deadline to move forward to the future without fully dealing with the past. I said I would not post any previous pics of myself once the year mark passed, but I was that pretty woman for almost 43 years, and she deserves more than me just packing her away after one year, so I will remember who I was and what I looked like until doing so becomes easier for me. You cannot heal from the past until you deal with the past. I am not who I was prior to April 28, 2013, and I never will be again. I am forever changed inside and out. People often say to me that I am the same Christy, not realizing that it is an insult to my journey to say that I am the same. How could anyone remain the same after what I have endured? I don't want to be the person that I was before. I want to be better, I want to be transformed, I want to be renewed. Something changed within me. Apart of me died that day and I'm still grieving that loss and waiting for the new me to be born, but I am not ready to let the original me go just yet, she was entirely too fabulous. I will not be packing her away anytime soon.

Monday June 9, 2014

Now I am 43...

I had my first kiss when I was 13

I fell head over heels in love when I was 14

I became a woman when I was...none of your biz ;)

I became class queen at 16

I went to college at 18

I met who would become the father of my children at 19

I experienced love at first sight at 21

I graduated when I was 22

I started my first business at 23

I bought my first of many houses at 24

I got married at 26

I became self-employed full time at 28

I had my first child at 29

I built my dream home at 30

I had the second child at 31

I had my first heart ache when she died

I had my third child at 33

I started my own real estate agency at 34

I got separated from my husband at 38

I got divorced and started grad school at 40

I was introduced to the splendor and beauty of me at 41

I also found my calling and my joy at 41

I lost it all when evil came in and took it away at 42

Now I am 43, and discovering yet another me

"I played by all the rules...and then they changed"

Now I am back at age 1...starting life again.

"The Curious Case of Christy Sims"

Tuesday June 10, 2014

I now operate with radical candor because drastic times require drastic measures. What happened to me was so drastic that I have to share it in a drastic and radical way. Whispering would not be appropriate; being burned alive should be shouted from the rooftops. To write is to fight, so I continue at the risk of being annoying. I will yell until someone hears me and helps me. I will yell until societal change occurs. I will yell with radical candor, genuinely, and with total transparency. When you get tired of me, take care of you and look away, but I am here to stay. I am telling my story in this radical way, hoping that I, along with others, get saved each day.

Saturday June 14, 2014

My internet was down at home, so I was forced to go inside of Star Bucks for the first time in over a year. I met a 22-year old version of *me* working at the register. She recognized me from the news and wanted to sit and talk with me on her break. I was in a hurry to get my blog up on my website, but I put it aside and sat with her. She was confused about her life, her career, and her relationship. She cried as she talked to me and I sat and listened...and then I told her everything that I wished that someone had told me when I was 22. I gave her every book that has helped me in the past few years. I told her to be kind to herself, to forgive herself, and to have as much fun as possible because one day she will wake up and be 43 like me. I spoke publicly this morning at an event in Dekalb County and then I counseled this younger version of me this evening, and it felt natural. I believe that these are my "whys". The women I spoke to this morning and this 22-year old are why He allowed me to go through hell, but survive it. I'm ready for my next surgery now. I will finally go home and pack.

Wednesday June 18, 2014

My ever changing face will change yet again in one hour when surgery #12 commences at 10:45am. I am hungry and craving the crab cakes that we had for dinner with Stanley and Iona Nelson yesterday. I want crab legs, steak, shrimp, butter pecan ice cream, Funyuns, Almond Joy, and a Diet Coke. This surgery is serious, but this hunger is real and it is not a game. All I can do is suck my fingers like a hungry baby. Sidenote: My anesthesiologist looks like Superman...seriously, he looks just like the actor, Christopher Reeve. The nurses and staff even refer to him as Superman, so when I'm prepping for surgery, I always asked to be sedated by Superman because he's super cute and his anesthetic cocktail is perfection. I'm out totally cold for surgery, but afterwards I'm not groggy and out of it for hours like I have been after previous surgeries. Anyway, here we go again. Dr. Spence will remove the skin above my lip and replace it with skin from my stomach. I'm not thrilled about it, but nothing can be worse than me having both cheeks grafted a few months ago, and at least he won't have to wire my mouth shut this time. I can handle this.

Thursday June 26, 2014

I can't even describe how I look right now. There are no appropriate words. Deep sigh...I will be back in hiding again until this heals. I'm delaying my next surgery until after October so I can attend events for Domestic Violence Month, plus I need a break from having my face rehabbed. This reconstruction process is taxing on the mind, the body, and the soul. I return home to Atlanta tomorrow. I'm still pressing onward...I am Courageous Christy, and I have earned that title.

Monday June 30, 2014

Being a professional counselor has its advantages and disadvantages during times in the valley. The average person just lets their blue days be blue days, but as a counselor I'm always trying to counsel my way quickly out of depression, instead of just letting myself feel what I need to feel. Sometimes I'm even still trying to help other folks, when I'm the one in trouble. Right now I'm going to lay here in bed with my blinds still closed for a bit and just feel. I have earned the right to have a few blue days. We all have.
Today, I am not okay. This is not okay. I have neither the energy nor the inclination – and I am too transparent – to even pretend that it is.

Ultimately, I know that I will be more than okay, and that will have to be enough for today. I'm going to pray, and pray, and pray until that future day, that I am truly okay.

Wednesday July 2, 2014

I am still bandaged and bruised, but back on my daily kid transportation duty: drop-offs and pick-ups. Mommy patrol never stops because kids don't give a flip about the fact that I just got my face sewn on, but if I didn't have them depending on me, I would be in a corner somewhere balled up in the fetal position sucking my thumb...lol. Thank God for kids!

Monday July 21, 2014

I cried every day for almost a year, then I woke up one day and decided to finally get help. I have never been clinically depressed. I am naturally happy and optimistic, but this is the crisis of all crises, and as a mental health clinician I knew that I had reached a dangerous low a few months ago when I became hopeless and couldn't get out of bed, so this counselor finally went to therapy. I also asked my doctor for mild depression meds. I needed them because I have children and I have to get up and go no matter what, and depression was hindering me. I am not better because of the meds only. Spirituality is the key for me. Medication just helps keep serotonin levels up so I can experience joy when it comes. I was courageous enough to seek help when I really needed it during the depression stage of my grief. Survival is my goal by any means necessary.

Wednesday July 30, 2014

I'm starting to take public speaking engagements now. People have been asking for months, but I wasn't ready before. I guess maybe this could be my new thing...public speaking and writing, two things that I'm pretty good at, but had not planned on doing anytime soon. I guess maybe God had different plans, and maybe I was setting my sights too low. I suppose maybe it's time to turn this test into a testimony. God can turn even the most horrific situation into something that can be used for His glory. I may or may not counsel face to face or sell another house again, but maybe I will be able to counsel hundreds or thousands with one speech. I'm following His lead. I don't know where I'm going, but I'm going anyway. I surrender...

Sunday August 3, 2014

Elon is starting middle school. She's nervous to be starting a new school, to be making new friends after having the same ones for 6 years. She wonders if she will get lost, if she will be accepted, if she will like her teachers. Her mind is just racing. She doesn't know yet how truly incredible she is, how her smile and personality can light up a room, how beautiful she is inside and out. I tell her, but I can't wait for her to figure it out for herself. It took me way too long to figure it out...

Monday August 4, 2014

My roommate at Emory rehab, Ola Mae Jackson passed away yesterday. This name and this life may mean nothing to you, but this spirit meant a lot to me. She was my roommate during my time at Emory, days after waking up from the coma. She is one of the few people outside of medical staff and four of my family members who saw me in the beginning. She saw my face days before I saw it for the first time, she comforted me when I cried at night, she prayed with me, she told me that I was still beautiful, and she did all of this while battling spinal cancer, being paralyzed, and in debilitating pain. She made me laugh when I felt like crying. She is one of my angels in the valley, a bright yellow tulip. Neither of us could walk when we met, and I could still barely see or use my arms, but miraculously I walked out of Emory after less than a month of rehab. Ola Mae never recovered, and now she is gone. Although I'm happy for her because she no longer suffers, it matters to me that she lived, and it matters to me that she died. She was my friend during the deepest, darkest part of my journey, and it was not by happenstance. An angel is receiving her wings.

Tuesday August 5, 2014

Bill passed away today. We found out two weeks ago that my step father had terminal cancer. He seemed perfectly well and in no pain two weeks ago. He went into the doctor for an exam, and now he's gone. Tomorrow is never promised. We will miss him, but he was a Godly man, and my mother is a Godly woman, so he will be in a better place, and she will have the peace that only God can give. All will be well. Strangely I have no sadness, just peace when I think of him because he had an incredible life. He traveled the world, he was loved, and he was happy. He died the way that he lived: quietly and peacefully, without pain, and surrounded by everyone that loved him. There is no better way to go.

...

My skin is tight, I'm funny looking, I'm uncomfortable, annoyed, agitated, and concerned about my mom. Complaining is not my thing, but transparency is and this is my current situation. I'm in a really funky mood...like wishing Drew would break his restraining order and walk through my door right now so I can go ape on him and "stand my ground" all over his face and body. I'm having a moment...it will pass...or maybe not.

Thursday August 14, 2014

I'm frying fish and just got instantly transported back to my grandmother's kitchen. I miss her. The original "steel magnolia," Doris Tucker, was so gangster. She was a prissy gun toting diva. She taught me to never sit with my back to the door and to never leave my drink unattended. She taught me the value of making my own money...and stashing it away. She taught me how to change a tire, how to fish. She took me to baseball games and wrestling matches. She taught me how to drive a car with one knee, while using both hands to light a cigarette (the 70s...ha!). She was a grandmother and a grandfather, and she stood in the gap for my parents. She bought all of my prom dresses and my wedding dress, took me on shopping sprees and taught me how to sew, knit, and paint, how to hustle and where to hide a gun. She never missed an important event in my entire life. She taught me the value of looking my best, even when I'm feeling my worst. She taught me to be both strong and feminine. My affinity for the homeless and less fortunate is the result of her taking me with her to help the homeless as early as 5 years old. She planned her entire funeral and lived her last days with grace and dignity. We spent time during her last two months, taking long walks and having long talks. Even in her death, she taught me how to live.

I'm sitting on the edge of my seat watching this crazy and interesting life of mine to unfold. I got my popcorn and Goobers, and I'm waiting on the climax. I'm wondering what characters will leave and who will stay. I'm wondering if this will end up being a tragedy, a comedy, or a love story. I am the author of my life, though, so I have some say in this, right? I'd better get about the business of writing it before someone else tries again to write it for me. I am the screen writer, the director, the producer, the costume designer, and the leading lady in my own life movie. Free will affords me this, but God owns the production company.

Wednesday August 20, 2014

You grieve more peacefully when you know that you have done all that you can possibly do for a person. The cancer was a curveball. My stepfather had a debilitating stroke just two years into his 22-year marriage to my mother, and my mom took excellent care of him for the past 20 years. I didn't fully understand her sacrifice and how truly incredible she is until this past year when she had to do the same for me. He was passionate about getting me back on my feet and he stayed well enough this past year for her to be able to be devoted to me, and as soon as I came home and could stand on my own, he finally laid down. She was patient and faithful, even though I'm sure at times he drove her nuts just doing old man stuff; he was much older than she is. But they never had a single argument in 22 years because they are both sweet spirits and they had harmony. She was his voice, his caregiver, his advocate, his best friend until he died, so she is grieving, but with peace, and that gives me piece.

Sunday August 24, 2014

I'm about to start back seriously practicing meditation again. I'm actually going to a real monastery with real monks and stuff to master it. It is so incredibly hard for me because of my kid-like attention span, but the only way for me to deal with this new and altered body of mine...is to get "out" of it sometimes and take mini meditative trips. My mind has ultimately saved my life. My ability to take mental trips got me through two months in a coma. My ability to use cognitive behavior techniques has helped me to ward off deep depression. I literally willed myself into seeing again, and I got my vision back even though the doctors said I would never see again. The mind is so powerful when we use it properly. My mind never accepted blindness, and it won't accept a life of disfigurement and deformity either.

143

Nope, not this mind of mine. We are only as strong as our minds.

Thursday August 28, 2014

Depression is real. Hell yeah I'm on medication...Zoloft 50 mg to be exact. I am not ashamed – I want to live. I'm a nationally certified mental health counselor with a Master's degree in matters of the mind. I was extremely happy, then someone that I trusted tried to kill me, nearly burned my face off and turned my life upside down. That's more than enough cause for depression, but I want to live through it by any means necessary. This life thing is not a game. It's hard enough without other folks coming in and messing it up. "Life for me ain't been no crystal stair", but I'm climbing anyway. I share so much because I care so much. This was never just about me.

Friday September 5, 2014

For the first time I awoke with the spirit of okayness (not a word, but should be). I typically wake up feeling some type of way, and it takes two hours of me praying and psyching myself out to be okay, but for the first time since the morning of April 28, 2013, I actually woke up feeling okayness...not happiness, but acceptance. I woke feeling like everything is gonna be okay, like greater is coming, like I'm truly gonna get double for my trouble, like I'm gonna be rewarded for my faith. Yep. I hope it sticks...the day is young.

I was talking to my sister-friend **Inger** about how kind people are to me now. I told her my life would be pretty good and I could really enjoy all this if I wasn't burned and uncomfortable, still had my pretty, and I still had my money. She brilliantly replied. "Well, if you weren't burned and uncomfortable, you still had your pretty, and your money, people wouldn't be so kind, and you wouldn't be going to see Oprah for free tomorrow." Isn't she smart?

Lord Jesus. I idolize no man or woman, but I'm so excited about being in the same building with Oprah that I can't sleep. I'm so proud of what she's done in one life time. I'm so proud that she's smart, thick, and brown like me. It's not her fame that I admire, it is the work that she has done for human kind that makes me so proud of her. I am proud of her willingness to be transparent and unapologetically imperfect. She gives so much of herself. Money means nothing if you don't use it to enhance the world...there are only so many things that you can buy with a billion dollars. Did I say that? That was some bull. A little known fact: I collect *O!* Magazines. Well, at least I used to – they're expensive...

Tuesday September 9, 2014

Our awareness of good is sharpened by the presence of evil. The contrast is necessary. If there were no darkness, how could we truly appreciate the light? Our bad days allow us to truly appreciate the good ones. Being a substance abuse and mental health counselor felt very much like battling demons. If you have ever seen an addict during active addiction, then you know what I mean. I think I may have been helping too many men free themselves, and the demons got pissed off and needed to shut me down, but it appears that God is expanding my territory. I am no longer counseling ten to twelve men in groups; next month I will speak to thousands of men and women. God is. He simply *is*.

Sunday September 14, 2014

The recent Ray Rice video of him beating his girlfriend has sparked a national conversation about the topic of domestic violence, thus I am flying to DC Tuesday to join a panel on the award winning Al Jazeera "The Stream" international news show to discuss the hashtag #WhyIStayed. I'm so glad this question is being asked on a global scale. It sheds light on the cycle of abuse, a cycle that most truly don't understand, even those who are experiencing it. Even a counselor like me, who actually studied the cycle. It is important to be careful not to judge things that we have little or no understanding of. Janay Rice likely has been in the cycle for many years and doesn't even know it, because the cycle probably includes so many instances of love, or what she perceives as love. That is the nature of the cycle: total confusion. One minute you're loved, the next you're hated. I was already in the cycle before I was a counselor, and becoming a counselor made me see it clearly...just not soon enough. Physical abuse is often the finale, as in my case. The emotional and verbal abuse are more silent and not always consistent. In fact, if you don't pay attention, you may miss it. You have to break a strong person mentally before you can break them physically. For example, he would remind me that I was "just" a Master's-level Counselor, and not a Psychologist or a Psychiatrist, and my response would be that if I wanted to be any of those, I would be because I'm smart enough. I chose to be a counselor because I want to help, not analyze and medicate folks. But why say something so negative at all to someone that you say you love? And then the next minute, they will praise you and say you're being sensitive or they were kidding. I guess I didn't feel like I was being abused because I'm a feisty lil chick, and I always stood up for myself, but negative words do sink in sometimes, and if you hear them over and over you will start to believe them. Oh, did I mention that Drew has no degree, when I have several? Insecurity...the root cause.

Tuesday September 16, 2014

This life I live – from being a counselor and a mom, to being burned alive, to surviving a coma and 12 surgeries, to starting a foundation, to becoming an advocate against domestic violence, to doing TV, radio, magazines, and blogs, and now an Emmy award winning international show – I just lived a lifetime in a single year. Basically, I need a nap, and Forrest Gump's mama was right: "life is like a box of chocolates; you never know what you're gonna get." I'm leaving the Al Jazeera interview and headed back to the "A" and to my babies. I'm riding home in my fourth chauffeured car in 24 hours. I must have been rich in another life, even though I'm not in this one...yet, because this feels strangely natural.

Friday September 19, 2014

I've been so busy. But, I'm trying to stay grounded and not get overwhelmed and swept away by this sudden flood of activity. Reminding myself that what is another person's priority and emergency is not necessarily mine. This was my lesson for the day, by the way. God shut all of my technology down for the past day, I believe, so that I could learn this lesson, could be still and listen and know that He is God. It is indeed my season, but everything in this season is not for me. Selectivity, quality over quantity, and impact are the keys. Because it is my season, I must make impact while I can. I don't need attention; I need change to occur, I need me being burned alive to not have been in vain, I need God to get His glory.

Tuesday September 23, 2014

I feel fall coming – that familiar morning breeze that puts me instantly at ease. It excites me, delights me because it is the prelude to something new…a new season, another chance to get things right. I am excited about my next season. I don't know what's gonna happen in it, but I will be alive to see it and that is good enough for now. I love the fall, and I am grateful.

Saturday September 27, 2014

This is my last quiet Saturday for a very long time. God even worked it out for the kids to be gone so I could truly be still. I actually got a full night's sleep last night for the first time in forever. The rest of this year is planned out for me. I can't believe that I've nearly survived the worst year of my life. I honestly didn't know how I would. I stayed busy. I found purpose in my pain. I cried a lot. I laughed a lot. I learned to ask for help, and I healed by helping. I became less of me and more of God. I encountered and reconnected with some truly amazing people. In spite of it all, I still have a good mind and a good heart. It's not over, but I will keep going. I really am courageous, and I truly am a survivor. I will rebuild my life…I will redefine *my* idea of beauty.

Tuesday September 30, 2014

There is healing in helping. I'm so busy trying to figure out how I can help other people that it leaves little time to think about how bad my own situation truly is – how bad I look, or how uncomfortable I am all day every day. Being burned is an uncomfortable existence, but I can't change it, so I focus on what I can change. I'm a counselor, so I do self-checks to make sure that I'm taking care of my own needs and not avoiding, but focusing on how I can help others really is helping me. If you want to get out of your situation, maybe try helping someone else get out of theirs too.

I truly believe that God will reward us over and above anything that we could ever imagine when we walk with blind faith. Nothing happened for an entire year, and some days it felt like He wasn't listening, but I kept going and I kept praying, and suddenly things are changing and coming in like flood gates. Not everything is good for me, but He has even given me the wisdom to have discernment in that. No matter what it looks like, please don't ever give up. I still don't know what will become of me and this funny looking face, but I'm living long enough to find out. Someone out there is thinking of giving up…don't do it.

Wednesday October 1, 2014

And so it begins: Domestic Violence and Breast Cancer Awareness Month. I need a nap just thinking about it. I'll be everywhere for the rest of the month. Yep, I am the woman who was in total isolation for an entire year, living behind a veil because my face was so disturbing. I didn't just get brave, I got better...I'm healing inside and out. No more hiding, my friends...see you soon!

Thursday October 2, 2014

1 in 4 women will be abused in some way at some point in their lifetime. That is a higher rate than breast cancer, which affects millions of women. 75 percent of all police reported cases of domestic abuse happen as a result of the person trying to leave the relationship. Indeed, my case was one of separation violence, I believe, because although I can recall several instances of what would be considered emotional and verbal abuse, I did not believe that I was in imminent danger. Abuse is about control, and a person can be completely docile as long as they feel loved or in control. The violence occurs when they are unable to cope with the loss of control over the other person, which is why leaving without a strategic plan is not always the answer. I thought backing away was the kindest thing to do because he had just lost his father. Ending it abruptly didn't seem necessary because we were not fighting. We only saw each other a few times a month, and we didn't live together, so it seemed easier to just back away and ween off of each other. Obviously my plan was not the right one.

Friday October 3, 30253

Therapy is a necessity for me right now and I have definitely found the right therapist. Dr. Kola is wise enough and spiritual enough to take this journey with me. I thought I needed a female, but what I really needed was a compassionate male counselor to balance out the evil that was done to me by a man. I gain new insight every time I go. Today I took responsibility for one thing as it pertains to what happened to me. I was unfaithful and disobedient to my own inner spirit. My inner knowing said that he wasn't right, even though he did so many right things. I always felt unsettled, unsure about the relationship. I was always running. My family never liked him, and honestly I cared about him, but I never really liked him either.

Your heart will lead you astray, your mind can fool you, but your spirit never lies and it will never lead you astray. Why? Because the Holy Spirit inside of you is a gift from God, His way of dwelling inside of us and protecting us from the enemy. I will never again deny it. No matter what I see, think, or hear. I take responsibility for just this one thing: being unfaithful to my inner spirit. Anything else belongs to the evil one; he owns this deed, not me.

Monday October 20, 2014

I have started back wearing my pretty clothes and high heeled shoes and doing my hair lately. I stopped when he destroyed my appearance, because I didn't *feel* pretty when I no longer looked pretty. Also because I've been in and out of surgery for a year and wearing yoga gear and sneakers was just easier. But I had to remind myself that pretty is not just a look, it is a feeling. I dress everyday now and try to look my best to honor the pretty girl inside of me. You cannot burn real beauty, real class, and real style...you just can't. I am beautiful, and so are you.

Thursday October 23, 2014

Mission accomplished. Chris, a technician with Total Contact, the designer of the $2000 burn compression mask that my friends and family and loved ones are helping me purchase to reduce my scars, just flew in from Ohio. He did a 3D laser scan of my entire face, and as I sat on the floor with my back against the wall in the busiest airport in the world, completely still so that he could get an accurate scan, I thought to myself, "Why hasn't one of the ten security guards passing by asked why we are sitting on the floor in an airport using scanning devices? Then I thought, "Medical technology is a trip." I'm not looking forward to wearing a mask 20 a day for an entire year, but I'm excited about having reduced scarring.

Thursday October, 2014

Today is Inger's birthday, so I thought it would be a good idea for her to go with me to record the Rickey Smiley Morning Show. What better way to start off the morning than with his silly self. He is so hilarious and so is his entire morning team. She and I arrived at the studio in downtown Atlanta at around 8:30 am and after waiting for 10 minutes, we were called into the studio to start the interview. I wondered how Rickey would handle such a serious topic and how he would respond when first seeing me, and his reaction was priceless. All I can say is that I just thank God that I'm not a hypersensitive person. Rickey's response when he saw me was simply "Damn!" He had not seen any pictures of me and he was totally shocked at how badly my faced was scared. His response to me hurt my feelings for a hot second, but then my silliness came through and I laughed. From that moment on I made it a point to have fun with the interview. The comedian in me came out in that interview and I actually had Rickey and his team laughing at times. I wanted this interview to be impactful, but not too heavy and sad. I wanted to enjoy my first time meeting this hilariously funny man with a big heart. The interview was only supposed to last for 10 minutes, but it went so well and it got so much feedback from listeners that they extended my segment to nearly an hour and it ended up being a two part interview that people are still listening to online. It was one of my most impactful radio interviews and it got national attention.

Sunday November 2, 2014

I've been speaking all of October and now it's time for me to settle down and have my 13th surgery. Dr. Spence is replacing my chin this time and I'm getting fitted for my compression mask at John Hopkins. I will be down for the next few weeks recovering from surgery.

My friend, Marques Neal arranged for mom and I take to a private Angel Flight to Baltimore this time. I'm both scared and excited, and mom is just terrified in general about flying on such a small plane. It's only a four seater and we will have to stop in North Carolina to catch the second plane to Baltimore. I'm feeling stressed, and running late getting to this little airplane, and my head hurts. I fed the kids but forgot to feed me. I know I forgot some stuff for this trip. Did I mention that I just packed an hour ago? Did I mention how much it kills me to see my kid cry every time I leave because she's scared I won't come back? Did I mention how much I dislike that Fordham dude? Hope my mood changes. It's a beautiful day and I could possibly enjoy this private flight if I were not so annoyed at the moment.

Two itty bitty planes and 8 hours later, we are finally here. Jesus, Mary, Joseph, Moses, and all twelve apostles took the wheel. I enjoyed it, and it was an experience, but for the sake of my poor mama, we are taking a commercial flight back to Atlanta next week. Thanks again Marques Neal and Angel Flight Soars....

Tuesday November 4, 2014

As I prepare for this 13th surgery, I am being forced to accept that I will never be with my cocoa butter friend again and I need to let him go. This is not my season for love. I need to set him free. He is kind and he wants to be here, but he is too whole and I am too broken.

Our spirits had not collided in many years, but he came back to me in my darkest hour as if he instinctively knew that I needed him. We are as connected as two people can be without ever touching or seeing each other. There are days when he is the only one on earth that can comfort me. We talk for hours and hours when the rest of the world is fast asleep. We delight in memories from the past, we relish in the present, and we explore visions for the future. The sound of his voice soothes me to sleep most nights and wakes me up most mornings. He edifies me, he empowers me. I am better because he lives, because he breathes. He is pure light and love personified. I see divinity in him and he reminds me of the divinity in me. For me he is like a vanilla scented home after a long hard day. He knows me – the real me, the original me. He knew me before any hurt or heartache, long before the world had its way with me.

He knew me when I was young and unsure; he knew me when I was innocent and pure. The sound of his deep and rich voice calms me and makes me feel safe, and the sound of his gregarious laugh is exhilarating. Wisdom drips from his lips like water from a faucet and I hang on every word because I trust him with all that I am. He knew me and loved me before I truly knew me and loved me. He sees the beauty in my scars; he makes me reach for the stars. He is my comforter, my counselor, and my friend. He makes me laugh out loud, yet makes me see the world in ways that I had never imagined before; he is both comedian and philosopher. I have loved him for many lifetimes and I will love him for many more. His love soothes me, it heals me, it comforts me and I feel free in his presence. He is as beautiful on the inside as he is on the outside. His heart is a work of art and he loves me in that agape way that only comes from God. Our love is real, right, and true. It is spiritual, it is profound and it requires no explanation; it is understated yet understood. He brings me joy and I know

for certain that God sent him to help me get through the darkest time of my life, but, it is time for me to deal with me alone. He has comforted me almost every day, but I cannot truly
grieve the loss of me because I sometimes get lost in the reverie of him, of us. I pretend that I am okay even when I am not so that we can have our precious moments, our fleeting bliss. He is my escape from hell. He helped me to become mentally and emotionally strong but now he must leave again like a thief in the night, quietly and peacefully. All I will have of him is our long and meaningful conversations during the midnight hours. He has enhanced my worldview without us ever laying eyes on each other in the recent years. I have not seen him in forever, but I am touched by his words and caressed by his spirit. What we have transcends time, space, and circumstance. Peace and joy have been my compass with him. Nothing about him feels wrong; he is grace and kindness, dignity and manhood, vulnerability and strength. He is all things that a man should be. He is everything to me. I pray to see him again one day in this life time or the next. I must let him go for now because this is not our season, but I hope that if he ever needs me that I can be there for him in the way that he has been here for me. I pray that our paths cross again during the light of the sun and not in the shadow of darkness. He is cocoa butter for my heart and for my soul; he is yellow tulips on a cloudy day…he made the pain go away.

Wednesday November 5, 2014

Dr. Spence is now partially retired, but he still has operating privileges here at the Good Samaritan Hospital. He and my new surgeon, Dr. Price will work as a team to replace my chin for surgery #13. I am not thrilled about their method of surgery. Based on the way she described the procedure, it sounds to me like I'm going to have a triangle on my chin. She says that the compression mask will help flatten it, but I don't know. All I can do is trust them at this point. I'm so tired of surgeries. I am so thankful that Dr. Spence stayed beyond his retirement to finish the bulk of my surgeries. He is such amazing man, and it goes beyond his skills as a surgeon. He has so much class, integrity and grace. I have grown to love him and Lori so much. I bought him a retirement gift and I'm going to give it to him when he releases me to go home next week. I hope that giving him a gift is okay. I feel like I owe this man my life and I want him to know that I truly appreciate how far beyond the call of duty he has gone as a surgeon. In spite of all the pain and in spite of the evil that brought about all of this, I am so thankful for the good people that I have encountered. The good balances out the bad. I believe that life is designed that way. I believe that God will always give us yellow tulips on our cloudy days. It is the tulips that let us know that God is real.

Friday November 7, 2014

I am so tired of having surgeries and I really don't feel comfortable with anyone other than Dr. Spence doing my burn reconstruction. I'm coming up here one or two more times after this. I was hoping this was the last time. At some point, I will stop letting these folks rip my face apart and just live my life. But it is not my nature to quit before I've done all that I could do, to be the best that I can be. A painful journey...but once you've been pretty, it's hard not to at least try to be it again. I didn't know how pretty I was until I wasn't. Enjoy your pretty, bathe in it, adorn yourself, and be pretty for me too.

As always after surgery, I'm feeling depressed. Mom and I are once again isolated in this room at the Holiday Inn in Baltimore. We have spent so much time here over the past year that the entire staff knows us by name. This has become our second home, but it is very different from my Henry County home. This has been a house of pain for me for the past year. I will likely always dread coming to Baltimore even after I've completed my surgeries because I associate it with so much pain. I'm depressed, but I'm only going to let myself be depressed just one more day, then I'm going to get up off my butt, take myself off these narcotics and plan to go home Thursday.

Chris made his high school basketball team, which was hard, and Elon has been preparing for her first cheer competition for the past 6 months. I have missed all of their stuff this year, but even if I have to sit in the back with sunglasses and a veil on and pretend I'm not their mama, I will see him play his first high school game, and I will see her first cheer competition. That's will happen. I've also decided that I'm not coming back up here for surgery. I'm taking my life back. Everything else will have to be done by God, the mask, and time. Tired of this phase now. Three more years with Chris before college. I'm not leaving them anymore. Over it...

Sunday November 9, 2014

I'm no longer depressed, just sitting here with my chin sewn on. My face looks like a quilt, but hey, I have nothing against quilts...no selfies for a while though. I will be incognegro for at least a month. Ready to get the heck out of Baltimore...got stuff to do. Four more days then I'm back in the "A"...back on Georgia clay.

Thursday November 13, 2014

I spent the morning in the Burn Unit at John Hopkins. This is the first time I've been around this many burned folks since I left Grady. It occurred to me that I've put more focus on me being a survivor of domestic violence and less on being a "burn survivor." I go to therapy, but I've never been to a burn support group to deal with the physical and emotional aspects of being burned, nor the limitations and discomfort on top of my appearance. I've been running from it by staying so busy advocating for DV. I'm a natural born advocate, but my working and doing has been contributing to me avoiding. I didn't want to be reminded and I've been avoiding other burn victims, but I had to deal with it this morning. It actually felt good to be in an environment where no one stared at my scars or even cared because they're scarred too, many of them much more than me. I met a guy with no ears (acid survivor, Henry Cole from Liberia...look him up; this happens to men too). It's time to go back to Grady and Emory, if only to say thank you.

I try not to "major in the minors," because there are too many big things to be concerned about for me to be sweating the small stuff. I must add that to things that get on my nerves...people who sweat every little damn thing. Jeez, get over yourself and take a trip into someone else's world for one day...just one. If you cock your head to the side and look at life from another angle, most of the stuff we worry about is manageable and is actually kind of funny. God is the ultimate comedian...try to plan your own life without Him and watch how hard He laughs at you.

Saturday November 15, 2014

Organized sports has been the best therapy for my kids. I believe in talk therapy and they did it for a few months, but the last thing my kids want to do is talk about what happened to us. I just keep them so busy that they don't have time to dwell on this stuff to long. I did everything possible to give them a happy childhood and do not want this past year to be their most prevalent memory. When they want to talk, we talk, and when they don't, we don't. Chris went to the World Series and played the best baseball while I was in a coma. They have literally played their way through this mess, and I like it that way...children heal through play.

Friday November 28, 2014

I'm a little afraid to say it out loud because I felt this same way at the end of 2012, but I'm feeling happy for no particular reason. Hopeful, and dare I say excited about the possibilities in this coming year. I'm thankful for the ever present Spirit of God that flows around me and dwells within me. Who I am as a human being has everything to with my keen awareness of the God in me. It has sustained me, and I am grateful.

Thursday December 4, 2014

I have learned to embrace, love and appreciate my "hallway" time, that quiet space between disaster and destiny that we often rush through, that space in our lives when there is nothing happening, when busybodies like me get bored and frustrated. I'm grateful for this quiet time. I'm using it to heal, learn, pray, and plan. I've learned to embrace the "hallway," to just *be*, and be good with that. I'm growing...

Tuesday December 9, 2014

I've been afraid to claim joy out loud lately because I was so happy and full of joy when evil came in last year and robbed me of it, but it is my birth right as a child of the Most High to live life abundantly. I claim, declare, and decree in the mighty Name of Jesus that by June I will no longer need donations personally, that my surgeries will be over, that I will be back in the position of "helper" and able to sow seeds into others because that is the position where I am most comfortable. I no longer have to be afraid because even when evil comes in, and it will, I am now stronger, wiser, and cloaked with the full Armor of God. I claim victory over the spirit of depression, over fear, over illness, over procrastination, and lack. I claim

155

that God's Will be done concerning my legal case, and I will accept the outcome, whatever it is, because no man's fate shall determine mine. I will be happy and free whether he is or not. I claim that all closed doors will be opened and all mountains will be moved on my behalf. I deserve peace, joy overflowing, and prosperity. I have earned it, and so have you.

Monday December 29, 2014

I stayed true to me and true to God...of that I am proud. I held on to that wavering branch in the midst of the storm, and I was not blown away...I was not blown away. Sandi Rivers advised me that the criminal trial may start as early as mid-April. I have decided to stop pushing against all of this and to allow the process to unfold. I will stand firm and not waiver. She is so full of integrity and grace, and I have learned to trust her word. If she says that we are going to trial this next year, then I believe her.

Dr. Kola recited a quote to me in my last session. He said, "Once God has anointed you as a headlight, being a tail light simply won't do." And I agree, you can never go back once He has elevated you, and once you discover who you truly are and the greatness within you is revealed, you can no longer deny it – you must continuously rise to the occasion.

I am still in Baltimore recovering, and all I can do in the hotel room is watch TV and write.
I value loyalty above all else, even love. I'm okay with you not loving me, but am not okay with you throwing me up under the bus. My favorite color is orange because it makes me happy. I meet every description of the Leo woman – every one of them. My favorite person is me. I am selfish at times, but never self-centered – there is a difference. I care about other people a lot, I just care about me more. My mask goes on first, then I will save you. I cannot fill your cup if mine is empty. I love confidence, but I truly dislike arrogant people, and I won't tolerate them. I will not counsel children because I have a weakness for them. I will never counsel child molesters, rapists, or acid throwers because I could never be objective with them. I would always want to rip their heads off. It would never work. I like being alone more than I like being with people. I am the moodiest person on the planet and easily annoyed. I'm 98 percent sure that I have ADD because I have the attention span of a 5-year old boy. I don't care much for

plants, mixed flowers, roses, or anything but yellow tulips and sunflowers. What's the point of fake flowers? I don't get it. My dream is to live on the beach and become a well published author. I really don't want to do anything but write and wear flip flops all day, every day. I have no particular type of man that I like. I prefer average Joes that are rough around the edges, but soft inside. He must love God and kids. I prefer that a potential mate be funny, have nice teeth, smell good, dress well, and show tenacity and confidence. I like imperfect and screwed up people because I find them interesting. My greatest fear is that I will die, and my life will not have mattered.

The person who broke my heart into itty bitty pieces when they left me was my daughter Kayla when she died. The ones that helped put my broken heart back together were Chris and Elon. The person that I'm the most connected to and who knows me the best is my son, Chris. I love food, sex, and sleep equally, and combining all three would be great. I am naturally shy, and although I can speak publicly in front of large crowds and on TV, small groups of strangers cause me anxiety and take me back to when I was a shy 8-year old. I honestly don't care if I ever marry again; being in love would be nice, but marriage not so much. I did it for 14 years. My lessons were learned. I think I'm good. I really don't like cooking or cleaning, but I do it because it just seems like the right thing to do, plus being hungry and filthy is not cool.

I believe in Christ and I also believe in reincarnation. It is inferred throughout the Bible and it was in there before it was removed by Constantine. I know that I have been here before, just as I know that God is real. I will either love you, like you or I will be indifferent to you, but I will never hate you, not even acid throwers. Hate takes too much energy. A short fly haircut and high heeled shoes makes me feel powerful and sexy. The moment that you figure me out, I will grow and change again. I'm a little too complex for most men. Being a spiritual being rather than a religious one makes more sense to me because I don't like being boxed in, and   I   prefer   inclusion,   not   exclusion. I love white BMWs, any model. In fact, I only buy white cars. I love music...any genre except folk and blue grass. I can roller skate like a pro and still own white skates with pink pom poms. And this is what happens when I'm locked in a room for days.

Saturday January 3, 2015

I am spiritual, not so much religious. It makes things less complicated for me. I can love all people of all religions, races, and sexual orientations without judgement or exclusion and without hypocrisy, whether I agree with them or not. Being locked in a box of religion is too confining for the divine and vast spirit that I am. I am just passing through, having a human experience, so I don't have time for all the dogma. I know that God is real because I've experienced Him for myself, not because I read about Him in the Bible. I read the Bible because it is a beautiful work of literature and it is a guide for my living, but I knew God before I could read. There was a time when I couldn't see any words, but God was still there.

Thursday January 8, 2015

A fragile ego will keep you from being great because you can never become great without constructive criticism and without acknowledging that you have room for improvement. I am not great, I am not my best self, but I work diligently at getting there every single day. The greatest people that I have encountered have been those that are the most humble, and those that understand the spirituality of imperfection.

Friday January 16, 2015

My next partner won't get the prettiest and sexiest me, but he will get the best and most beautiful me. I now have the experience without the excess baggage. My journey has taught me well; I have learned from my challenges and mistakes. I actually learned more about marriage and relationships after divorce than I did during my long marriage. I got married young and didn't know what the heck I was doing half the time. I loved him well, but it was based on the way I viewed love, instead of the way that he needed it, and vice versa. We typically give people what we want instead of giving them what they need. Assumption is the worst form of knowledge. When it comes to men, sometimes all you have to do is ask, "What is it that you want and need from me, baby?" and they will tell you. Women can be more complicated, but asking us is the first step. Here's a tip: We love it when you learn what we need without asking because you've been watching us so closely and you just know. I am qualified now. I have the knowledge, the experience...and the skills. ;)

Friday January 23, 2015

I write about the "hallway" a lot. I think I'm coming out of it this year, and that's kind of scary because I can never go back to yesterday. I can never be subpar or ordinary again. Laziness won't fit in this part of my journey. Ultimately "it is our light, not our darkness that most frightens us." Success is scary because it requires more of who we are not. We can hide and be lazy in the dark, but we cannot hide in the light, especially when it is shining directly upon us. We cannot hide. Yep, I'm feeling insightful...

Saturday January 30, 2015

I am a work in progress. I am ever changing, ever growing into a better me, physically, mentally, spiritually, and emotionally. Human beings are just like flowers – we are either growing and changing, or we are dying and decaying. I am growing and changing literally every day, and the moment that I stop is the moment that I die. I don't ever want to have it all figured out. The joy is in the journey, the lessons keep me longing, and the mystery is fun.

Wednesday February 11, 2015

He hurt me because I was a good woman, not because I was a bad one. I wasn't leaving because I was being beaten; I was leaving because I was unhappy with him. You don't need any other reason to leave any situation. It is our birth right as children of the Most High to have joy and peace, and I didn't have it with him. Even though he destroyed my outside, at least I have that joy and peace now. What was my crime? Why did he do this? Because I chose myself over him. I was not my best self with him; I am my best self now. After years of putting others' happiness before mine, I finally chose me. Joy and peace is our compass, so if we don't have those, then we are not headed in the right direction.

Saturday February 14, 2015

I am finally open to love again. I woke up early this morning thinking about my man, my future man that is, and I got excited at the mere possibility of him. I don't know who he is yet (or maybe I do), but I am already in love with his soul, with his essence, and with his heart. I feel as if he's somewhere nearby or someone that I have encountered before. In any case, I can feel him preparing himself for me. I wish I could tell him that he is enough, that he is already perfect for me because I am not perfect, and that we will grow together. I got elated just now at the thought of loving him to the depth and width and height my soul can reach. I'm excited about the one that God is preparing just for me. What a happy soul this man He has chosen for me will be! I will love him infinitely.

I am so excited about falling in love again because it's going to be so good. It will be a love that is based on what is real, what is right, and what is true. It will be pure and deep and rich, and non-superficial. He will see my scars as works of art and as evidence of the miracle that I am. He won't need me to fix him because he will already be whole and so will I. It will be based on wisdom and discernment and grace. It will be spiritual and divinely designed by God. I am excited. I hope that he is too.

My desire is to fall in love with a good and spiritual man and spoil him rotten (in a good way), and live at the beach or by the water with him, and make love at least three times a day (sometimes by the water). I want to see every beautiful place in the world with him. I want to pray with him and see plays and listen to music with him, and discuss life and books and how we can change the world. What I want is to set him free whenever he needs to be free, and for him to always choose to come back to me because I am the one that sets him free. What I want is a love that transcends time, space, and circumstance. What I want is the love of a soul that is so profound that when I see it in a future life, I will recognize it and we can resume what we started here. That's what I want, Universe. I will wait...

I had an epiphany. I realized that I've been fighting like a bulldog for domestic violence because it's the part that people understand and talk about the most. It is the thing that I can do something about and change. It is the hot topic right now, but it's not the part of my journey that almost broke me because I didn't know I was in an abusive relationship until it ended. Drew wasn't beating me, and he never broke my spirit. The hardest part of my story is the one that most people will never be able to relate to, and that is going from being pretty for 42 years to being completely burned and disfigured. I live a lonely existence even though I'm surrounded by people…I am surrounded by *beautiful* people. I don't personally know anyone else who has been burned to this extent. This is a completely different dynamic, totally separate from DV. I only went to a burn support group once before. I believe that I have avoided them, but lately other burn survivors have been reaching out to me, and I found someone that gets it today, someone with a courageous soul like mine, but who has had to be this kind of courageous since she was burned at two years old. I found a new friend who understands. This is what I needed: someone who understands what it is like to be different and unpretty.

Friday February 20, 2015

This human experience is a trip, especially when you are as keenly aware as I am that we are merely spiritual beings having a human experience. There is indeed bliss in ignorance sometimes, but knowing that this whole human experience is temporary and full of tests that are designed merely to enhance us spiritually is comforting for me. It is why I can tolerate even the cruelest inhumanity. It is our knowledge that we are *in* this world, but not *of* this world that separates us and makes us special. I am not a human being that has spiritual experiences; I am a divine spirit just passing through, gathering what I need to draw nearer to God's brilliant light. We must walk it through it, but it is easier when you are aware that ALL things, even the really bad things, are designed for your spiritual growth. I forget sometimes because the human experience was designed for us to forget sometimes so that we can learn. The real lessons are learned in the valley on the cloudiest of days.

Monday March 16, 2015

I just decided that I don't even want all of the life that I had back, and this is a powerful decision. You cannot move forward until you except that you can never go back. My life was safe, quiet and comfortable. My desire to go back to being pretty, regular, suburban Christy has been holding me back from being this new woman that has risen out of those ashes. Before I blended in with other people, now it is impossible for me to blend in, I can't go anywhere without being noticed because of my scars, so I may as well embrace that I will never be ordinary again. I will never blend into the crowd again. The woman that woke up from that coma is more bold, more fearless, more dynamic, more inspiring, and extraordinary. The woman that went into the coma was great too, but she was nowhere near reaching her highest and best potential. I can be bold and fearless now because I have already faced the worst things in life imaginable..

Friday, March 20, 2015

As hard as I tried, I didn't feel pretty today. Pretty is not just a look, it is a "feeling". A feeling that every woman should have. Most days I find a way to feel pretty in spite of my scars. I love wearing my beautiful clothes and keeping my hair and make-up done. I keep my pretty feet polished and on point. Most days I can tap into that pretty girl inside of me, my former self...but today I could not...I even took the mask off for a long while so that I could play in my make-up, and I re-polished my toes ...but it didn't work...I could not find her today....today was not a pretty day. Vanity has no place in my journey because I have never been vain. I never thought much about my looks until they were so drastically altered and now I look back at old pictures of me as if I'm admiring a pretty friend that I once knew. Today, I'm not referring to inner or outer beauty, today I'm referring to that "feeling" that a woman should have...that feeling that most women take for granted. I always feel beautiful because I know the definition of beauty...and I am beauty defined. But some days, I just want to feel "pretty" and I could not find it today....maybe tomorrow. Some days I just miss her...

Monday, March 30, 2015

I am flawed in every way imaginable. I have ADD, I am unorganized, I am a procrastinator, I'm a bit lazy at times, I'm scattered and all over the place at times, I am forgetful, I am defiant against adulthood at times, 18 was a good age and sometimes I'd rather just shut it all down and go home to my mama. I am too proud. I am a nonconformist, if everyone is doing it then I'm doing the opposite. I am a good mother, but I am unconventional and I could be a better one. I am feisty and moody, and easily annoyed. I am the opposite of what most imagine me to be. I have great moments, but I don't have it all together most of the time. I am my own worst enemy. I love God with all my heart, but I don't read my Bible or go to church as much as I should. I'm really not the best Christian, in fact I've been running from holiness and chased by evil my entire life...and sometimes it catches me. I believe that evil seeks me out because of my great potential for holiness. I am forever faced with moral dilemmas. I am a sinner a hot mess by all accounts. I am as far from perfection as one can be. But, I am good to my core and God has anointed me, my life, and everything that I touch. I am shocked and amazed by His grace.

Wednesday April 15, 2015

Last year at the one-year mark, I blogged about what happened to me on April 28, 2013. I cried and wrote from sun up 'til sun down while I was in Baltimore recovering from having both cheeks sewn on. I was in so much pain, mouth wired shut, and I couldn't eat for 2 weeks. I purged and released that day last year. This year, I'm doing it a little different. I am celebrating on the 25th, and then on April 28th, I will do something meaningful, but more private. I'm still trying to figure out how I want to handle the day that I lost my face. It kind of feels like someone died. I grieve for my former self the same way that I grieve for my baby girl, Kayla. I don't ever want to forget her, although I was blessed with another daughter, and I never want to forget the original pretty face that God gave me, even though He is blessing me with a different face and a new life. I will always honor her, and I will always honor the "original" me.

Monday April 27, 2015

I never thought that I would get here – certainly not in less than two years, or before completing my surgeries, or before going to trial, but tomorrow is April 28th and I am here. I am OKAY. Okay doesn't mean that I still won't cry like a baby some days. But at this 2-year mark, I have decided that I would rather be burned and alive, than pretty and dead. That being said, I shall now walk boldly into my destiny. I AM OKAY.

Friday May 8, 2015

I had an eventful spring season, but I've been so busy that I have not had time to journal as much. So much has happened. In March, I attended the APCA college convention and gave my largest talk and received a standing ovation, the only one the entire week. As a result I was booked to speak at various colleges throughout the nation during Domestic Violence Month this October. Cherry Collier referred me to her friend and speaking coach,

Sean Smith and he coached me towards having my first major talk. I have spoken several times during the past few months, but after October I will be a professional public speaker. Just before I went on stage at the convention, Sean called me and put Lisa Nichols on the phone and she inspired me. She told me to make sure that I ended my talk with a question for the audience to think about and I did just that. The Universe is so amazing, just one week prior to me being in Jacksonville and speaking with Lisa on the phone, I had posted a video clip of her from the Steve Harvey Show and she was speaking about us rescuing ourselves and being unapologetically successful. Her message empowered me and I told myself in that moment that I would meet her one day. That was in March, well just last week Inger and I were in California celebrating Lisa Nichols, renown public speaker, co-author of Chicken Soup for the Soul, and teacher of the "Secret" birthday with her and other friends. Sean invited me to a conference they were hosting and Lisa celebrated her birthday during the conference. It was serendipitous meeting her two months after seeing her in that video. My life is so strange and interesting.

I have decided to unplug from the public until the trial. For the next two months I am doing nothing but praying and meditating and spending time with Chris and Elon. Going to trial with Fordham feels like going into spiritual warfare and I will need to be strong spiritually, mentally, emotionally, and physically. I have been going non-stop for two years and I am burned out in every way. I need this down time before trial. Drew is a liar and I already know that he will do and say anything to avoid going to prison. I am preparing myself for him and his attorney attacking my character and integrity. It is his defense attorney's job to do everything possible to keep him out of prison, so I am expecting a fight. But, I have two very powerful things on my side. I have an all-powerful God and I have the undeniable truth. I will not worry, but I will be prepared. I'm going to do the Master Cleanse as a fast until trial to strengthen me mentally. I am always more clear with my thoughts after this cleanse. I am preparing for war, a war that I have been waiting for two years to take place. I will be ready.

Saturday May 9, 2015

I got what I needed this week. It is true that our Creator knows each and every one of us individually and knows what each one of us needs. I am burned, I am scarred, and I am wounded emotionally, but I am still a woman. I still have needs, wants, and desires as any human being naturally would. I have not been physically involved with any man since I was burned. When he took away my face and body, he took with it my sexiness, my femininity, and my confidence. I have always been comfortable with my body and with my own sexuality. I loved my nakedness. I wasn't the finest woman in the world, but I have always had a sexy curve to my body that men seemed to enjoy. After being so terribly scarred, I no longer felt pretty or sexy. I could no longer stand to see myself naked and I felt quite certain that he had succeeded in making me undesirable to any man. Not only am I facially disfigured, but I am scarred on over forty percent of my body. How could any man find me sexy and desirable ever again? It is not the sex that I miss, it is the intimacy. It is the touch and the feeling of closeness I get from being with a man that I care about. I missed being touched.

I have wanted the comfort and love of a man. I am very comfortable with being alone, but I have never been isolated to this degree in my life. I am deeply spiritual, but I am still human, and sometimes I want the warmth and positive reinforcement that only a man can provide. I needed the passion and the feeling of being wanted, appreciated, and adored.

The poor man must be blind because I look hideous, but he looks right through the scars. He looks at me as if I am the most beautiful woman in the world. He said that he could not see my scars due to the depth of his love and concern for me.

We have only been friends, but he always seems to instinctively know exactly what it is that I need. He knew that I was celibate and he knew that it was not sex, but intimacy that I needed. I didn't tell him, he just knew. He has been there during my deepest valleys and pulled me out of some truly dark moments. I had grown to trust him, to trust his genuine love and concern for me. He had earned my trust – he was my friend.

I walked into the candle lit room on the 14th floor of the Sheraton Hotel in

North Atlanta. There were candles and rose petals everywhere, but how did he know? I never told him that this is what I like, that I love surprises, that I love romance. We have never dated, and he has only been my friend. He touched me, kissed me, and caressed me as if I was the beautiful woman of his dreams. In that moment I forgot about the scars because he kissed every scar and he looked at me in a way that made me feel like the old me, the fine and sexy me. It was pure intimacy. It was beautiful. It was spiritual. It was love. It was what I needed when I needed it. He reminded me of the me that I once was. He reminded me of the me that I again hope to be. He reignited my woman-ness. He gave me what no one else could in that moment because he had earned my trust and there were no walls between us. I allowed myself to relax in the moment and to be vulnerable. I allowed myself to dwell in the now – no one else existed but us in that moment. He helped me to realize that I am still a fabulous and sexy woman, and that I am still capable of captivating the heart of an amazing man. He brought me back to life again as a woman, and he made me realize that I would one day have true love again. I am grateful that his time and schedule allowed him to be with me when I truly needed him. He touched me, held me, and nurtured every inch of me; every scar was honored. He knew that I was not ready to be sexual with him or any man and that it was not sex that I missed and needed, it was love and intimacy, and that's exactly what he gave me.

A Letter to My Inner Child

Dear Christy,

I am so proud of you. You are beautiful, you are smart, you are kind, and you add so much value to this world. Your love of writing and poetry means something, stick with it and do not quit. Please forgive me for allowing you to grow up so fast. You missed some pivotal steps in your development my love. You have caught up through trial and suffering. But I could have saved you so much heart ache if I had shielded you from experiences that you were too young to process. Falling in love at such a young age was exhilarating and loving him was everything at that time. But you had sex way too young, you were not ready. Your heart was broken way before you even knew how to love yourself. He loved you before you loved you and it should never be that way. The men in your life defined you because you had not yet defined yourself.

Your dad loved you to best of his ability, he just didn't know how to show you because he was so young and was still developing and discovering himself. You looked for your father in each and every one of your relationships with men, but you never found him. My love, you learned too late in life how to fill your own voids and to not allow yourself to fill the voids of other broken people, and you have paid dearly for this. I wish that I had told you how special you are back then, and that you don't need anything or anyone outside of yourself to feel complete. You are enough, you have always been enough. I wish that you had laughed more, traveled more, and experienced more of the world. I promise to take you to every interesting place in this world. I promise to allow you laugh when you want to, and to cry whenever you feel like it, no matter who is watching. I promise to nurture you more and to put you before anyone else, including Chris and Elon because I know that if I take care of you, you will in return take care of them.

No matter how bad you may feel at times; please know that your minimum is someone else's maximum. You are incredibly blessed and beautiful, and you have everything that you need inside of you to be happy and fulfilled. Let joy be your compass. Let peace be your purpose.

I love you, Christy…the wiser version of you

What I Want My Children to Know

You were wanted, planned, and loved long before you were conceived. In spite of it all, life is good and you are safe to love and to trust. You are both smarter than I was at your ages, so you will likely make better decisions than I have. You don't have to make all of your own mistakes, just learn from mine and your dad's. People will typically tell you who they are the first time you meet them, believe them. You have unlimited potential because you serve an unlimited God. You are worthy, you are important, and you add value to this world. Follow the direction of your joy. You will know that you are headed in the right direction because you will feel joy headed in that direction. It is okay if you don't reach your destination because the joy is in the journey. Be quick to listen and slow to speak. Assumptions are the worst form of knowledge, just ask people what they want and tell them what you need from them. Be positive, every word that you speak should be a reflection of who you are. Spirituality is more expansive and inclusive than religion, but gain your own understanding of God. Cry whenever you feel like it, and laugh whenever you feel like it. Do what is right, even when no one is looking. Love people the way "they" need to be loved, instead of the way you want to love them. Everyone in your life is not meant to stay, some of them cannot handle the level of the greatness that God has planned for you, weed them out graciously. It is okay to be selfish sometimes as long as you are not self-centered. Love yourselves first and most. Lastly, I am proud of you both. I see you as the amazing and divine spirits that you are, thank you for coming to this plain and choosing me to be your mother. You are the first thoughts on my mind in the morning and my last thoughts before I fall asleep at night.

I love you both infinitely.

-Mommy

Saturday July 11, 2015

I met Drew at Pets Mart while picking Sam up from the groomers. He nearly talked my ear off while standing in line waiting for the cashier to check us out. Within two minutes, I learned that he was from Miami, he had two boys but always wanted a little girl, and he had a dog named Chaos. After a few minutes I zoned out and began planning dinner in my head as he talked. I prayed the cashier would hurry so I could get way from this chatter box. He was annoying the hell out of me. He seemed arrogant and boastful. He was short and bald with a gap in his teeth, but, nothing turned me off more than his excessive talking. I cannot stand a man who talks too much. After a few minutes of listening to his chatter, he mentioned that he was a real estate investor and because I was a real estate agent at the time, he had finally said something that peeked my interest. He went on to talk about how many houses he had flipped and sold between here and Miami.

He went on for a few more minutes and I was finally free because the cashier was finally checking me out after what felt like an eternity in line with him. As I walked away, he gave me his business card and asked me to call him. I never mentioned that I was a real estate investor and broker because based on first impression, this was not someone that I ever wanted to see again, or someone with whom I would want to do business. Nevertheless, against my instincts, the real estate agent in me reached inside my purse and gave him my business card.

He called me two days later, but I didn't recognize the unidentified phone number so I did not answer. I listened to his voicemail and as I contemplated returning his call, an eerie feeling came over me. It was as if that decision to return his call would be life changing. Eventually, I called him back and we talked for a long time about real estate and business in general. He seemed less arrogant and annoyed me far less than when I first met him. A few days later, I met with him and began to show him property, but he never actually bought anything. He showed me a large tract of land that he had bought and as we sat in the car on the vacant land, we talked and learned that we had a lot of weird things in common. We discovered that we were both Leos, we both had sons who were the same age and both

169

allergic to peanuts. We both drove white Ford trucks from the same dealership. Both of our maternal grandmothers were deceased and both named Dorothy. Both of our mothers were Geminis born in May, and both of our fathers were born in July. Drew and my father are both born on July 24th, the day after Chris's birthday. It went on and on and suddenly we were communicating nearly every day. He treated me like gold in the beginning. Every interaction was fun and exciting. He would somehow figure out where I was and just pop up there. He catered to my every need. He brought me flowers and handwritten cards. He said that he wanted to marry me and give me everything that I have ever wanted. The rest of the world became a distant memory. I became lost in him. Overtime we became closer and closer and more dependent upon each other. I met his kids and he eventually met Chris and Elon. They both looked at him as if he had two heads or something. They did not like him from the start. He was overly friendly with them, but they couldn't stand to be in the same room with him, so I kept them away from him as much as possible.

Over time, we began to argue about little things. He identified every one of my flaws and made it a point to highlight them. He criticized my cooking. He criticized me as a mother and said that I was too soft with Chris. He was angry that my kids would never accept him. He would become infuriated whenever he thought that Machon and I were getting along too well, so he would call Machon and start disagreements with him and thus drew a wedge between Machon and me. He said negative things about my close friends and would always come up with a reason why I should spend time with him instead of them. I felt increasingly more isolated and controlled. He would become infuriated if I was too friendly in the presence of other men. He would grab my arm beneath the table during dinner with his friends if he wasn't pleased with the way I looked at them or if I looked too long, yet he would intentionally flirt with other women in my presence in an attempt to make me jealous.

If I gained five pounds he would let me know, but if I lost ten pounds then he would say that I needed to gain it back because my butt was getting too flat. He was nurturing and catered to me and cooked for me, but he would become angered by the smallest things. I felt at times as if I was dating twenty different men at one time because his moods would change so often and so quickly. We broke up at least twice a month because being with him felt bad half of the time, but he would cry and beg and bring flowers and write love letters and beg some more, and I would go right back to him. Our sex life was the best part of our relationship. It was sensual and spontaneous and fun. We were passionate and uninhibited and totally addicted to each other. He knew every inch of my body. Our lovemaking was rhythmic and spiritual, and we were always in sync as long as we were having sex. He knew exactly how to please me, and I knew exactly how to make his toes curl. He was addicted to me and I to him for a long time. Eventually all we had in common was sex. I could not stand him outside of it. He knew that last month and that last weekend that I was finally resolved and leaving him for good because I no longer wanted to have sex with him. Sex had always been our common ground, but I had finally lost interest. The relationship was over and he know it. His last tool of control over me was no longer working.

Our relationship was always precarious. I never expected it to last forever because it was so unhealthy. I just could not seem to get away from him. For so long I was blinded and confused by him because he was equally as loving as he was verbally and emotionally abusive, and thus he kept my head spinning all the time. One minute I felt loved, and the next minute I felt hated. Eventually I found a way to back my way out of loving him by listing every negative thing about him. I literally wrote down all of his flaws, even the smallest things, and I would read the list as often as possible. This is a method that I'd read about in the book *The Portable Therapist*, and it actually worked. I backed my way out of loving him and finally released his irrational hold over me, the hold that I now realize was an ungodly soul tie.

Sunday, July 12, 2015

Pastor Paula White speaks often of ungodly soul ties. A soul tie is an emotional bond or connection that unites you with someone else. You can become bound to a person through your soul. Not all soul ties are bad. A soul tie is deemed ungodly when there is evil attached to it, or when there is sin involved, or when the relationship is outside of the will of God, or sometimes all three. An ungodly soul tie is tormenting, confusing, and miserable; there can be no consistent peace and joy in that bond. The only way to break a soul tie is through fervent prayer, because only God can overrule the presence of evil.

I didn't know that I was in a cycle of abuse until I awakened from a two month coma completely and utterly broken by a man who was once my lover and my best friend. Thinking back, there was nothing extraordinary or remarkable about him, nothing that was even cause for a pause. He was charming at best. I was attracted to his brokenness, I suppose. He was a tortured soul, always struggling between good and evil. The counselor in me thought that I could make him better, but instead he made me my absolute worse. I wanted to witness him reaching his highest and best potential, but, he used my own heart as a weapon against me. Evil hits us where our treasures, are and my heart is the most sacred part of me. I thought that I had control of my life and of that relationship, but I was wrong. I was a professional helper, but I could not help myself because I could not see my own picture from within my own frame.

Drew wooed me with candlelit rooms filled with rose petals. He sugar coated insults with gifts and trips and "I love you." He would lift me up and tear me down within the blink of an eye. He assaulted me not with a fist, but with subtle words and gestures – so subtle that most of the time I couldn't see or hear the evil, but I could feel it. I've been engulfed with love and kindness my entire life, so this was foreign to me. I didn't understand it. He masked controlling and possessive behavior with statements like, "I'm just worried about you; that's why I call you twenty five times a day." If I even looked at another man, that would be a two hour long argument. I stayed with him beyond my own happiness because he had convinced me that I was the primary source of his. He did not love me – he loved the idea of me. He was addicted to the way that I made him feel, but for me there was no longer any love. All that was left was a sense of responsibility mixed with my ever growing disdain for him. In the end, I could not stand the sight of him. I prayed that he would find interest in someone else so I could be released and have peace.

I wanted him to be well and happy...just not with me. We never lived together, yet our spirits collided all day, every day. I was so depleted after every conversation with him. I felt hostage to his emotional needs. There was always something that he needed me help him get through, always something that made me feel guilty about leaving him. We fought and made up, fought and made up, over and over again. He knew in the end that I was finally gone, that I had checked out emotionally because I didn't care enough to even disagree with him anymore; I had become indifferent. As I said, I no longer desired him. Even his lies and deceit became amusing to me. I was no longer phased by his crocodile tears. He could cry on a dime without any emotion, which I still find so odd. Only sociopaths can do this. There was no God in that relationship; in fact, it separated me from God. I felt more disconnected spiritually during that time than I ever have felt in my life. I didn't have the spiritual covering over me; I did not feel that hedge of protection that I've felt my entire life. I felt out of God's grace, as if I was encapsulated by sin.

That relationship was unhealthy, dysfunctional, and co-dependent. It was bred out of deep rooted fear and insecurity, and not just his. I am woman enough to own my own stuff. As confident as we believe that we are, we all have our insecurities and fears. There was a time when his control felt like a security blanket, a blanket that he ultimately used to smother me. He identified every void in me and tried to fill them, but you cannot fill another person's voids when you have a zillion pot holes of your own. He did not change; he was always evil – I had just never seen evil that close before, so he was able to dress it up with suits and expensive cars, with great sex, with humor and excitement. He was spontaneous, edgy, romantic, and fun, but very mean at times. We had no trust, so I felt like I was sleeping with the enemy, an enemy that I had this irrational loyalty and concern for because in the beginning he reminded me of love and of a time when I was young and free. He reminded me of my first love. However, it was not love. Love does not make you mad, sad, guilty, or regretful. It doesn't give you anxiety and fear. It doesn't make you want to scream and run away, it certainly doesn't throw acid in your face. Love is freedom and kindness and grace, it should make you better as a person. Love sets you free, yet prays for your return. It was never love, it was an ungodly soul tie.

Monday, July 13, 2015
Jury selection

Drew will finally have to face a jury. It is after 2 pm, and jury selection has been going on all morning. I will be sequestered throughout the trial and only allowed to be in the courtroom for my testimony, the closing arguments, the sentencing, and the conviction, so there was no need for me to go to court today. I am just sitting her awaiting Sandi's call to let me know that a jury has been selected so that we can start trial tomorrow. I will be the first to testify at 9 am in the morning if the jury selection is completed today. My emotions are all over the place. I am nervous and I am angry after seeing the CSI reenactment last week, and actually watching them prove how he did all of this. I broke down at my house as I watched Henry County reenact the crime over and over for five hours last week. Sandi said that this is what she was waiting for. She said that I needed to see this and attach to what happened and feel the anger in order to be a good witness. I have been avoiding thinking about this as much as possible, but she is right – I needed to see this. I needed to get mad as hell so that I can fight back tomorrow.

They showed how every scar got on my body. They used a man Drew's height (5'8) and a woman my height (5'2), and they were able to prove that the incident happened as I said it did. My cell phone rang, and it was Sandi. She said the twelve jurors were selected. There were nine Caucasian women, one Caucasian man, one African-American woman, and one African-American man. Sandi was not pleased with the jury make-up until I explained Drew's personality. She thought that a jury of more black women would be more favorable to us because I am an African-American woman, but I knew that this jury was perfect because Drew is charming and charismatic and able to con women, but he would have less of a chance of doing this with a jury of 9 white women, mostly middle-aged. I was pleased with the jury make-up. I am ready to face him tomorrow. I am afraid, but am equipped with the armor of God.

Tuesday July 14, 2015 trial begins

Mom and I arrived at the courthouse an hour early. We sat and prayed and listened to gospel music before walking in. We were both ready. We were placed in a private room until I was called to testify at approximately 10 am. My stomach was in knots and I felt as if I were going to lose everything that I had for breakfast. I tried to calm myself by breathing and slowing my heart rate. Lorraine lead me to the second floor courtroom and she sat with me on the second row, where I awaited to be called to the stand. Mom was required to stay in the witness sequester room in case she was called to testify later in the week. Surprisingly, for this to be such a public case there were very few people in the courtroom except for the media. I preferred it this way because I knew that I would have to discuss the intimate details of our relationship. My dear friend Stacie Savage was the only person in the courtroom on my side that first day, and I was comforted by her being there. LaNese and Jonell were there the remaining days of the trial, but Stacie was there all day every day from beginning to the end. We were never close friends before this happened, only classmates, but I can say with certainty now that Stacie is a true friend. I will never forget how much she has supported me.

I was finally called to the stand and sworn in by Judge McGarity. I remembered him as the same judge who signed Machon's and my divorce decree. He is known for being stern but fair. I sat on the witness stand about ten feet from the jury, and Sandi began questioning me. I have watched a zillion episodes of Law and Order, so I knew to only answer what was asked and to make eye contact with the jury throughout the questioning because they would be the ones deciding his fate, and they needed to connect with me emotionally. Sandi asked me to recount my entire relationship with Drew from the beginning all the way until he doused me. She asked me to recount the details of April 28, 2013. She asked me so many questions that I can't remember them all. I just answered as clearly and concisely as possible. I began to cry out loud as I remembered the pain of that day. All of the emotion of the past two years came down on me as I sat there finally on the edge of receiving justice. It felt like justice just to be able to finally sit in front of a judge and jury and not be treated as if I were crazy the way Detective Brand had treated me. I remember him once telling me that I should be more careful the way that I break up with someone next time. It was as if he was blaming me for the acid attack.

At any rate, after Sandi questioned me, I was then questioned by defense attorney Chapman. He tried to refute all of the answers that I had given Sandi in an effort to paint me as a liar, but it did not work because I was telling the truth. His questioning was aggressive, but nowhere near as harsh as I have seen on Law and Order. I expected that he would be so hard on me that I would break down and cry, but it wasn't like that at all. Chapman was relatively gracious for a defense attorney. Sandi did an excellent job of anticipating his defense so that I could answer questions during her examination. There was not much left for cross examination. All that remained were the false statements that Drew had told Chapman and the police, and I was able to dispel every one of them. Lies are no weapon against the truth. I testified for nearly an hour. I never made contact with Drew, but I could see with my peripheral-him shedding crocodile tears throughout my testimony. It was all an act. I have seen this man twice before in a Fulton County courtroom, and he showed absolutely no remorse. I looked much worse then than I do now. I am convinced that he is a sociopath.

I left the stand and was taken back to the sequester room, where I remained throughout the day. This was a full day of testimony. After my testimony, the firefighter EMTs Phil Baker and James Kress testified to what they saw the day of the incident. Their testimonies were nearly as important as mine because they were the only ones to see the crime scene before Drew cleared everything away. I learned after trial that they were the ones to report this as a crime, and they followed up several times, but Henry County police would not act on the calls until the media became involved. I never knew that these men had been advocating for me until after the trial. I am sure there are so many things that I still don't know about how this case was handled.

After Kress and Baker, my brother Quinn testified to Drew's harassing behavior after the crime. He testified to what he saw in my house the next day and I heard later that his testimony was the longest and most riveting. I have yet to see all of the trial footage, and I don't know if I ever want to see all of it. Stacie said that it was so difficult to watch the trial that being sequestered was likely best for me.

The next witness was the locksmith that Drew called to my house while I was in a coma. His testimony was needed to show that Drew had access to my home because so many of my personal items were missing, including my laptop. The last witnesses of Day One were Crime Scene Investigators Katherine Brown and Jennifer Green. They both testified to the reenactment at my house, which revealed that the crime happened exactly as I said it did. They proved that it was bowl with a wider opening instead of a coffee cup as Drew had stated. It was inferred that Drew rearranged the scene of the crime as we awaited the ambulance.

Day One concluded and I went home. Drew was the first witness of Day Two of the trial. I stayed home that day because it made no sense to sit in that sequester room all day feeling isolated and claustrophobic. Sandi said that if she needed me to return to the stand, she would call me at home, so I stayed home and washed clothes while watching "Martin" and "Sanford and Son." I got several calls from friends and family who were watching Drew charismatically lie on the witness stand, but I didn't want to hear about it. I have been hearing him lie for years, and I know that he is a master manipulator. His life now depends on him lying better than ever before, so why would I want to hear that? I protected my psyche by focusing on everything but the trial. I know the truth and I stand firm on it. After Drew's testimony, Sandi called CSI investigator Jennifer Green back to the stand to refute Drew's testimony, and from what I heard later, she was able to tear his testimony apart with the evidence.

An acid expert from Georgia Tech was also called by the prosecution to testify about the Clean Shot product and how dangerous it is. He said that he would not want to handle that product even wearing gloves, and the labels clearly state how dangerous the product is. He said that you should never pour it out of its original container and you should never handle the product without gloves. Drew was recalled on the last day of testimony and the closing arguments began. I chose not to hear Chris Chapman's closing arguments because I knew that it would be based on Drew's lies, so I waited and returned back to the courtroom for Sandi's closing arguments. She was amazing. I so admired her as I sat there watching this brave and fierce women calmly and intelligently rip Drew's entire case apart. She even brought up the question that Sam was not present when the EMTs arrived, though he had been there with me all morning. Drew putting Sam away prior to the acid attack showed premeditation. She asked the question, "Where was her doggy that never leaves her side when all of this was happening?

Friday July 17, 2015
The Conviction

We have been fighting for two years, Andrew Lee Fordham, Jr. was finally found guilty of attacking me with sulfuric acid. Tonight he will spend his first night in jail for this crime. Sentencing is July 23rd, Chris's 16th birthday.

Saturday July 18, 2015

I woke up feeling much lighter this morning because I have one less task to complete. A task is what it was. I don't hate Drew, and I have never been vengeful. Vengeance is God's territory. I just had an overwhelming need to see good win over evil. I believe that he is evil. You have to be a sociopath to not only methodically plan an acid attack, but to stand over me and watch the flesh burn off my bones, which is what he did. He showed me no mercy. He wanted to make sure that I would be so unattractive that no other man would want me. That was his goal. I haven't been able to discuss the details of this case, but I can now, and I'm glad to finally tell it all, including the true nature of that relationship and how mentally and emotionally abusive it really was, I believe that it will both shock and heal some people. Evil is just as real as God is, but it will never win. This fight I've been fighting for over two years was for the woman he would have hurt next, the women he's hurt in the past. This fight was for every silent victim of violence, the ones who don't have the media following them like I do. I did it for that person being abused right now as I speak. I did it for her, I did it for my kids, I did it for *me*. Correction: *God* did it, for this battle was never mine. I will never rejoice in this man's demise. – I am too gracious for that, but I feel so much peace knowing that he will never hurt another woman.

Wednesday July 22, 2015

The sentencing is tomorrow and Drew will likely get a lot of time in prison. I've said several times that I have yet to forgive him, but I do not hate this man in spite of all the pain he's caused me and my family. Hate requires more energy than love, and he doesn't deserve that much energy from me. What I feel for him is nothing. I neither love nor hate him – I am indifferent. I know that I will have to forgive him eventually, but God is still working on me. I'm not that good of a person, and I haven't gotten there yet. It's more difficult to forgive someone who has absolutely no remorse, who smiles and laughs confidently in court, who cries on cue, and who continues to hurt you by lying on you even after he's tried to destroy you, but I also know that forgiving him is not for him, it is for me. I'm just not there yet, but I do pray for Andrew Fordham's soul, and I hope that God shows him more mercy than he showed me as he watched me burn alive.

Acid attack is one of the most heinous and inhumane acts known to mankind. Over 1,200 women were attacked this same way over the past two years, and most of the attackers are never brought to justice. When they are, they rarely get more than three or four years in jail. Most of the women attacked are beautiful and were attacked because they refused a marriage proposal or a man's advances. The women often commit suicide, or in countries like India, they are abandoned by their own families because women have little value, and life is even more hopeless for a burned and disfigured woman. So I suppose I did all of this for them too. Justice for one is justice for all.

Thursday July 23, 2015
The Sentencing

Drew was sentenced today to two counts of aggravated battery, one for disfiguring me and the other for blinding me, and one count of aggravated assault for using the acid as a weapon through the actual throwing. After hearing statements from his mother, his two sons, from Drew himself, and finally hearing my victim impact statement, Judge McGarity sentenced him to a total of 40 years, with 20 to serve in a medium security prison and the remaining 20 years to serve on probation after his release. He is eligible for parole and I will be present at every parole hearing for the next 20 years. My hope is that he serves the entire 20-year sentence, which is very likely since he is already a three strike felon. It is finally done. I am so grateful to Sandi Rivers and Kip Jarrard and everyone who fought for justice in this case. I will do a press conference here at the courthouse, then I'm doing an interview at another location with Inside Edition, and then we are going to the Atlanta Fish Market to celebrate Chris's 16th birthday.

Drew was indicted on April 10, 2014, which is my brother's birthday. He was sentenced to prison today on July 23rd, Chris's birthday, and he will serve his first day in prison on my father's birthday, which is also Drew's birthday, July 24th. The universe is at work.

Sunday, July 26, 2015

For a long time, I thought that he had won. His goal, I suppose, was to destroy my beauty and my entire life, to make me completely and utterly undesirable to any other man. I elected not to address him in court because he has no remorse and my words would not have mattered anyway, so I looked directly into the eyes of Judge McGarity and I directed my victim impact statement to him. But, what I want Drew to know now is that he did not succeed. He did not take the best part of me, and I will be more than desirable to the man that *I* find desirable, because I don't want just any man. It will take a special man to walk with the anointing that God has placed upon me – a man with his own anointing. A very special man.

Saturday August 1, 2015

I finally got to meet James Kress and James Baker, the firemen who saved my life on April 28, 2013. To say that I love and appreciate these men is an understatement. They had the wisdom to strip me down and rinse me with rain water after Drew let me sit and burn for more than 13 mins. By the time they got there, it was too late to save my face, but the chemical burned through my chest to within 2 cm of my heart, and their quick response and God allowing it to poor down raining at that moment is what kept me from dying that day. They were the first responders who reported this as a crime, and then they later followed up when police did not investigate because they saw the scene that first day, before he cleared all the evidence. They saw what I could not see, and what the police never saw and ultimately their testimony helped to convict Drew. I thank God for them and it was an honor to meet them. Now it is time for me to go back to Grady and Emory to thank them all. It will be emotional, but it is time.

What I Know for Sure…

Happiness shines through you, it makes you look better, prettier, sexier, younger even; I'm convinced of it. I'm diligently working on being happy again. From now on, I will always follow the direction of my joy, even if it's in the opposite direction that everyone else is going, because even if I don't get there, I will have enjoyed the journey. I realize now that the qualities that made me an affective counselor, such as objectivity, non-judgment, empathy, compassion, and genuine concern for others almost cost me my life. In my personal life, I will be more judgmental because some people need to be judged. I will now listen to my inner voice the very first time that it speaks to me. I will never again care for a person to the level that it becomes a detriment to me. If I want to leave, I will leave immediately. If my kids don't like him, he must go. If I want to be alone, I will be alone and not apologize for it. A healthy relationship should make you grow. When there is no more growth in any situation, it is time to end it. I will be more aware of insecure people because they can hurt you. Love should feel good most of the time – if there is more pain than joy, *run*! As I know better, I will do better.

Turning the page…

It is July 23, 2016, Chris' 17th birthday. Drew was sentenced to 20 years and sent to prison on this day one year ago. He now resides in Wheeler Correctional Facility in Alamo, Georgia. Chris was 13 and Elon was 10 when this man changed our lives forever. I was robbed of my face and of life as I knew it, and my children were robbed of a part of their childhood. Time was stolen from us that we can never get back, but we are healing and

181

moving forward. Chris has been playing baseball all summer and is preparing to go into his senior year of high school, and Elon is now in love with volleyball and will be in eighth grade this year. I am preparing to go back to my counseling career, and I have been touring and speaking for the past year since the trial. I have appeared on television many times, and my story was recently featured in major publications in South Africa and the United Kingdom.

Machon lives within two minutes of us and still watches over us like a guardian angel. None of us will ever be the same again, but our children are smiling again and that brings us joy. We are all adjusting to a new normal with the understanding that we are not meant to be who we once were. It would be an insult to our journey if we were not transformed by all of this. We are all more guarded and leery of people, but our hearts remain open and receptive to love. My mom is still grieving the loss of Bill, but she is resilient and steadfast and she will endure. My brother and I are closer than ever before, but I can still see the anguish in his eyes from not being able to protect me from so much harm. My father and I have the relationship that I have always wanted. I can see in his eyes how proud he is of me, but I can also see the pain in his eyes because he has forever lost his pretty little girl. As a family we are surviving evil. We are all stronger and wiser and we love each other infinitely.

Sometimes you have to lose everything, including yourself, in order to truly find yourself. There is absolutely nothing like the feeling of being on the other side of hell. I still have more surgeries to go, but I have resumed life and I can now go out in public with my head held high. I can handle the stares from strangers – they no longer bother me because I know how far I have come from living behind the veil. I will have other trials in my life and I will never truly be done with this one because my condition is lifelong, but I know now that I'm strong enough to conquer whatever happens in this life.

This is my story, but it is only a chapter in the book of my life. What happened to me does not define me. I am not a victim of domestic violence, I am a survivor of it. I lived to tell my story and I will spend the rest of my life speaking on behalf of every victim who did not live to tell theirs. I am still disfigured, and even after numerous surgeries, it is not medically possible for me to have my previous face again. I am scarred on over 40 percent of my body from skin grafts and donor sites, but overall, I am physically, mentally, emotionally, and spiritually healthy. I can say with certainty now that I was a beautiful woman on the outside, but I can also say with certainty that it was not my greatest asset. He failed because my real beauty was always on the inside. I will never have the face or the life that I had before, but eventually I will adjust and I will love this new me that I am meant to be. He bent me, he battered me, and he altered me

physically, but he could not destroy my spirit.

I have endured indescribable pain, and I have lost so much of myself, but I have learned so much. I have met so many incredible people and experienced so many amazing things. I am known around the world for being courageous. I have so many possibilities that I did not have three years ago. I was in a long dark hallway with two closed doors at each end. I was stuck between my past and my future, caught between disaster and destiny. Today, I am still in that hallway, and the door behind me is closed forever, but there is now light in the hallway because the door ahead of me is wide open. All I have to do is learn a bit more, grow a bit more, and pray a bit more, then I can walk right on through that open door. I have no clue what's on the other side, but the door is finally open, so there is now possibility and that is all that I require to keep moving forward. And by the way, that old acquaintance that Prophetess Iantha mentioned two years ago? The one that she said would come back into my life and change it for the better? Well, he just walked back into my life. I don't know what will become of us, but there is now also the possibility of love.

Yellow Tulips on A Cloudy Day

In spite of all the pain along the way, He sent yellow tulips on a cloudy day
I had no clue at forty-two that I would be a different me by forty-three.
What I want people to know when I leave this earth?
Is that I was good to my core since the day of my birth
I loved God first, then me, then my family, then the world
I knew my life had purpose even as a young girl
I want them to know that I never gave up, I never quit
I stayed on my knees, I prayed, I got through days by using my wit
I want them to know that I was a writer, a poet, and a fighter

While in the valley of the shadow of death, through peril and strife

When my spirit was dark and gray and I could not find my way

God sent friends and strangers with grace and mercy

He sent yellow tulips on a cloudy day

ABOUT THE AUTHOR

Christy Sims is a public speaker, an author, a nationally-certified Clinical Mental Health Counselor and a survivor of and advocate against domestic violence. She holds a Bachelor Degree in Marketing from Georgia Southern University and a Master's degree in Clinical Mental Health Counseling from Mercer University. Christy is the first reported case of an acid attack in the state of Georgia. To date, she has undergone 13 surgeries to reconstruct her disfigured face and body, and her personal struggle has propelled her to advocate and support other survivors of domestic violence. She has spoken out vigilantly about her experience via numerous public speaking engagements and media outlets, including V-103, WAOK,104.7, The Tom Joyner Morning Show, The Rickey Smiley Morning Show, Channel 2 Action News, Fox 5 Atlanta, CBS Channel 46, 11 Alive News, The Atlanta Journal and Constitution, The New York Daily News, Jet Magazine and Headline News.

Her story went international when she was featured on the award-winning Al Jazeera international news show "The Stream," which reached 280 million viewers worldwide. She has also been featured in numerous blogs in the U.S. and internationally. Her story was featured on the T.D. Jakes Talk Show, Inside Edition, The Doctors, TBN and, most recently, People Magazine South Africa as well as The Guardian and Woman's Own Magazine in the UK.

Christy's story has touched the lives of millions around the world and possibly prevented other cases of domestic violence. She received the Fortitude Award on April 12, 2014, the Courage to Act Award on October 11, 2014, and, most recently, the Community Empowerment award and the Uplift Award for her work in advocating against domestic violence. In 2015, the Fulton County Commission honored her with the official Proclamation of April 25th as "Christy Sims Appreciation Day" in Fulton County, Georgia.

The Christy Sims Foundation is a 501 c3 non-profit organization focused upon the prevention, awareness, and education of domestic violence.

My Yellow Tulips

My mom, Elaine, my brother, Anthony, my dad, Thomas, my step dad, Bill, the father of my children, Machon, my children, Chris and Elon, Connie Sims, Angela Gail Witt, Laura Madison, Imari Tucker, Jorden Tucker, Cami Tucker, Anthony Tucker, Vanessa Tucker, Odis Williams Esq., Tanya Mitchell Graham, Esq., LaNese Harris, Jonell Myers, Crystal Drake, Charles Sperling, Francis Monroe, Warren Mitchell, Joseph David Smith, Maggie Kempken, Laci Texter, Dr. Robert Spence, Lori Taguding, Dr. Walter Ingram, Dr. Doris Armour, Dr. Benjamin Stong, Inger Jackson Garnett, Michelle Hoxie, Dr. Cherry Collier, Dr. Quinn Gentry, Judiffier Pearson, Stanley and Iona Nelson, Prophetess Iantha Taylor, Pastor Jannette, Pastor Maya Taylor, Felicia Bright, Johnnetta McSwain, Denice LeSure, Mellendy Che' Gore, Deborah Gibson, Ravry Sloan, Rod Heard, Geary Woolfolk, Ronita McAfee, Sandi Rivers, Lorraine Bunn, Kip Jarrard, Evelyn Roberts, Kat Brown, Jennifer Green, Lisa Rayam, Tom Reagan, Ryan Cameron, Rashan Ali, Tammy Joyner, Priscilla Shirer, Bishop T.D. Jakes, The Doctors Show, Holly Tuckman, Jejuan Hall, Tharon Stephens, Tamara Hill, Daphne Jordan, Walter Jordan, Dante Charles, Shanti Das, Shatrice Jenkins, Sabrina Jenkins, Lisa Smith, Stephanie Williams, Tami McRae, Davashay Page, Desiree' Robinson, LaVonda Green, Lisa Black, Stacie Savage, Monica Davis Smith, Jan Kendall, Jay Allen, Tony McGee, James Dubose, Cheryy Collier, French Spencer, Sean Smith, Stephan Scott, Necole Gibson, Rodney Oglesby, Tabitha Amos, Bunnie Jackson-Ransom, Marvin Arrington, Jr., Maynard Jackson III, Wendy Jackson, Jennifer Alvarez Tucker, Amira Alvarez, Drexina Nelson, Nurse Regina, Grady Memorial Hospital Burn Unit in Atlanta, GA, Emory University Rehabilitation Center, Atlanta GA, Nellie Myers, Ginger Carter, Ralph Heard, Jr., Basil Lue, Ralph Long, III, Dr. Carry Roseberry, Trevor Roseberry, Sandra Roseberry, Sherri Allen, Sharri Thomas, Maceo Heard Jr., Keith Gulley, Carol Jones, Jennifer Madison, Marlon Nichols, Karli Butler, Sandra welch Welcom, Gina Rochelle, James Beasley, Morris Williams, Candice Gallet, Deidra Freeman, Antonio Johnson, Vincent Robinson, Elaine Young, Tonja Talley, Felecia Butler, Shunda Webb, Andrea Lytle, Danita Powell, Turan and Beverly Smith, Chaplin Janet, Gail Holmes, Kandice Mitchell, CGP, Stacey Chandler Franklin, Monica Moody, Sylvia Atchison, Marc Michael, Donna Ballard, Yolanda Nicholson Shorthouse, Marques Neal, Ola Mae Jackson, Sue Harris Vaughan, Sandra Gresham, Angeron Whatley and everyone else who has donated to me, prayed for me or helped me along the way. Thank you.

51874404R00121

Made in the USA
San Bernardino, CA
03 August 2017